FIND YOURSELF

THE

SPIRITUAL

ENERGY

Dr. Anthony Martin

Author ~ Scholarship ~ Leadership

Motivational Speaker

The Kingdom Culture Fellowship Ministries
& Christian Self Publishing's

Contents

This Book is Dedicated To:

THOSE
WHO HAS AN
EAR LET THEM
HEAR

Introduction

In spite of the many differences among Christians, Jews, and Muslims, they share a fundamental belief in God as compassionate and just. As a result, those communities have often nurtured people of extraordinary kindness and courageous commitment to justice. In contrast to the deep hatred that obviously inspired the September 11 attacks on the World Trade Center and the Pentagon, the vast majority of Muslims, like their Jewish and Christian counterparts, are appalled and sickened by terrorism, and utterly repudiate the mass murder of innocent people. Why then do some members of those same communities believe that it is their moral obligation to wage aggressive holy war, even to annihilate innocent people in God's name? What aspects of their scriptures and traditions tend to support violence against "infidels"? What ethical principles--religious and non-religious--can we affirm in response to those ideas and the atrocities that they sometimes engender? Religion is clearly not the only catalyst of total war and other forms of indiscriminate violence. People seem to be able to invent all sorts of   rationales for mass killing without feeling the need to cite the will of God. For example, just a few days prior to the September 11 attacks, two young men from the Sacramento area each killed half a dozen people, apparently out of personal revenge. And some of the most appalling atrocities in history have been rooted not in religion per se but rather in racial or class hatred. There may even be a genetic tendency in our   species, like that of our chimpanzee relatives, to attack and kill others for no reason except that they aren't "one of us. One of the Mosaic commandments prohibits murder (Exodus 20:13). Why is murder wrong, other than its obvious conflict with love of neighbor (Leviticus 19;17-18, 33-34)? Essentially because people are made in the image of God (Genesis 1:26-27, 9:6). One might infer from that idea that no killing of persons would be allowed at all, that the concept of human beings as made in God's image would entail strict pacifism, an absolute duty not to kill people. But that is not what the ancient Hebrews concluded, since many offenses were subject to capital punishment, a form of killing (see examples in Exodus 21-22). So perhaps we might interpret the image-of-God idea to mean, all persons have a basic right not to be killed, but they can forfeit that right if they commit a serious enough crime. This would be consistent with punishing only those guilty of crimes (Deuteronomy 24:16) and limiting the use of deadly force to the defense of innocent others or oneself. This is probably what most Jewish people would affirm today.

Introduction

One might infer from that idea that no killing of persons would be allowed at all, that the concept of human beings as made in God's image would entail strict pacifism, an absolute duty not to kill people. But that is not what the ancient Hebrews concluded, since many offenses were subject to capital   punishment, a form of killing (see examples in Exodus 21-22). So perhaps we might interpret the image-of-God idea to mean, all persons have a basic right not to be killed, but they can forfeit that right if they commit a serious enough crime. This would also be   consistent with punishing only those guilty of crimes (Deuteronomy 24:16) and limiting the use of deadly force to the defense of innocent others or oneself. This is probably what most Jewish people would affirm today. But religious violence can take on a particularly intense and ruthless character, if the objects of that violence are seen as blaspheming or insulting God, as the enemies of God or God's way narrowly conceived. The problem of indiscriminate holy war is particularly difficult for Judaism, Christianity, and Islam to eliminate from within because it's so deeply rooted in their scriptures and traditions. The same religious traditions that affirm God to be compassionate, merciful, and just, also include more disturbing claims that promote religious hatred and intolerance, and sadly have provided a rationale for aggressive holy war. We need to face these things head-on. Questioning the moral justification of holy war leads, moreover, to troubling questions about the legitimacy of some basic theological claims and the authority of foundational religious scripture. But collective punishment and indiscriminate war were also commanded or approved in the Hebrew Bible, especially in cases of idolatry. The first of the Mosaic commandments prohibited the Israelites from worshipping any other gods but Yahweh. God demanded purity and strict obedience, and idolatry and blasphemy were punishable by death (Exodus 20:3, 5).   Non-Israelites who lived within the area believed by the Hebrews to have been promised to them by God were seen to pose a great temptation to them to abandon their faith. This led them to justify the slaughter of entire communities (Deuteronomy 20:10-18). And their holy wars eventually inspired similar wars many centuries later by Christians who admired Old Testament warriors like Joshua: "[Joshua's army killed   everyone in Jericho], both men and women, young and old, oxen, sheep, and donkeys.... Joshua defeated the whole land... he left no one remaining, but utterly destroyed all that breathed, as the LORD God of Israel commanded" (Joshua 6:21 and 10:40).

Introduction

In the **Islamic** tradition, there is a similar mixture of values restraining war along with others promoting it. The Qur'an repeatedly refers to God as compassionate and just. It also says that "there is no compulsion in religion", submission to God must be freely chosen, not forced. The Qur'an urges Muslims to use "beautiful preaching" to persuade people to accept Islam and to "argue nicely" with Jews and Christians who are seen as worshipping the same God as their own. This is probably the attitude of most Muslim people today. Jewish and Christian communities have often been tolerated and protected under Muslim rule. Muhammad was said to have practiced non-violence early in his prophetic career but soon came to believe that God commanded the use of force, not only in defense of his growing religious community (Qur'an 22:39-40) but also in the form of offensive jihad to expand the territory of Islam. The word Jihad, by the way, means struggle or effort. Jihad can refer to the struggle of the individual Muslim to conform his or her will to Allah's, or to a peaceful effort to persuade others to accept Islam. But Jihad can also mean holy war. In fact, there's a sense in which the only completely just war in Islamic terms is a holy war since it has to be approved by proper religious authorities and waged to defend or promote Islam or the Muslim community. In spite of the Qur'anic statement against forcing religion on others, Muslim leaders have sometimes threatened to kill unbelievers if they did not accept Islam. Although Islam spread to some parts of the world like Indonesia mainly by means of "beautiful preaching," much of its expansion elsewhere was due to offensive war, first by Muhammad to unify Arabia, then by his followers in conquering Palestine, Syria, Iraq, Persia, and parts of India, North Africa, Spain, Turkey and the Balkans. Now, Muhammad and his successors did express some important moral rules for fighting holy wars: women, children and the elderly were not to be directly attacked (though they could be enslaved). Jihad was not supposed to be total war involving indiscriminate killing (in spite of what Osama bin Laden had claimed). But Muslim leaders were permitted by Muhammad to kill all captured soldiers and male civilians if they were not Muslims or had abandoned Islam.

The fact that you might be a civilian or a soldier who had surrendered didn't necessarily protect you from being killed after a battle against Muslims was over. Thus, Islam traditionally did not have a generic principle of noncombatant immunity though many Muslim leaders today uphold such a principle. Of course, Muslims are probably as prone as Christians and Jews to seeing in their holy scriptures only what they want to see, ignoring other passages that contradict their preconceived beliefs. Someone inferring a mandate to wage indiscriminate, offensive war from Qur'an 9:5, "Kill the idolaters wherever you find them," could only do so by ignoring the particular historical context of that passage, verses elsewhere that urge defensive and limited uses of force only, such as Qur'an 2:190, "Fight in the path of God those who fight you, but do not transgress limits, for God does not love transgressors," and numerous other verses praising patience in adversity and nonviolent preaching. Turning to Christianity, its early history was characterized by a fairly strict form of pacifism. That approach slowly gave way to an acceptance of violence in defense of the innocent. And sadly, some Christian leaders eventually came to advocate force against heretics and infidels, and even total war in the interest of defending and expanding the faith. In spite of the loving and peaceful tenor of his teachings and example overall, Jesus did occasionally show anger, as when he confronted the merchants in the Temple (John 2:13-16). Some New Testament passages also appear to accept the institution of the military, if not explicitly praise it: Roman soldiers who met Jesus, John the Baptist, Peter and Paul were not asked by any of them to abandon their vocation (Luke 3 and 7, Acts 10 and 27). (Arguments from silence are notoriously weak, however.) There's even a passage where Jesus seems to permit his disciples to carry swords, and by implication to use them in some situations, though that passage appears only in Luke 22 and is very ambiguous. Jesus also claimed the authority to call on legions of angels to protect him, but held back because it would conflict with his sacrificial mission (Matthew 26). Paul in Chapter 13 of his letter to the Romans declared, "Let every person be subject to the governing authorities. For there is no authority except from God, and those that exist have been instituted by God." He who is in authority "is the servant of God to execute the Law of the Land on the lawless."

But Jesus also set very high ethical standards for his followers, including an unbounded willingness to forgive wrongdoing, non-retaliation against evil, and love of enemies (Matthew 5). Three of the Gospels say that he rebuked one of his disciples for using a sword to defend him at his arrest. Most of his early followers seem to have interpreted Jesus' commands to prohibit all uses of force by Christians, even in defense of the innocent. Paul echoed Jesus' nonviolent message in his letter to the Romans, Chapter 12: "Repay no one evil for evil ... never avenge yourselves." Over a century later, Tertullian argued that holding public office and being a soldier would inevitably require actions forbidden to Christians; in his view, "It is more permissible to be killed than to kill." Hippolytus thought that Christians should not join the army; but if they were already in the army, they must disobey orders to kill. Although some Christians served as Roman soldiers during the Church's early history, a very significant shift in Christian thinking about war occurred in the fourth century when Emperor Constantine began to use the Roman state to support the Church. Christian pacifism was from then on to be strictly for clergy, monks, and nuns; lay Christians would now be obligated to discipline. Jesus' commands not to resist or retaliate against evil, although Christian love entailed a duty to use discipline to defend innocent third parties--indeed, a Christian who refused to prevent injury to another person would be as bad as the one who inflicted it. The focus of Christian moral concern from the act of violence to attitude of the agent: Christians should love their enemies, even as they repel them with deadly force! In effect, Roman military virtues for Christian purposes: risking one's life to defend the empire became courageous, just and noble for Christians. Augustine believed that there should be moral limits on war. Even in cases where Augustine considered war to be the lesser of evils, he regarded killing as ultimately tragic, always requiring an attitude of mourning and regret on the part of Christians. Partly due to his influence, throughout most of the medieval period, killing in war was considered a very serious sin. If a Christian soldier killed an enemy soldier, even in a war that was considered just, the Christian soldier would have to do penance for the killing, usually by fasting and prayer for a year or more. Beginning around the ninth century, though, another important evolution of Christian thinking occurred.

Introduction

Killing unbelievers was actually declared by popes Leo IV and John VIII to be spiritually beneficial for Christian soldiers: Their sins could be erased if they killed in defense of the Church. In the year 1095, Pope Urban II launched the First Crusade, urging European leaders to rescue the Christian holy lands from their non-Christian occupiers. He referred to the Muslims who then controlled Palestine as an "unclean nation" that had polluted Christian holy places. Killing Muslims became itself a form of penance for Christians for remission of their sins. Moral rules governing the conduct of war were abandoned, and unlimited tactics were permitted. No one was immune from attack by Christian crusaders; whole cities were slaughtered. Tragically, some advocates of aggressive religious war can still be found today in Judaism, Christianity, and Islam. What they cannot legitimately claim, though, is that their position is the authentic expression of their faith. Every major religious tradition contains ethical principles that are incompatible with total war. People of all faiths can agree, that innocent civilians should never be directly targeted, that indis-crim-i-nate weapons and tactics should never be used against military targets in ways that would produce large civilian casualties, and that captured soldiers should not be tortured or executed but treated humanely. This would be the hope that in our present crisis of civilian death in our communities across this great Nation of the United States. We can resist the temptation to execute the "indirect" and or "direct" killing of large numbers of noncombatants as "collateral damage" dictated by "military necessity." But take a necessary step toward achieving greater compassion on such things is the recognition and accountability of the troubling lives and the value of life embedded deeply within the scriptures and religious traditions. In many Christian worship services, it is a common practice for someone to read aloud a passage from the Bible, and indicate the end of the passage by saying, "The Word of the Lord is Blessed," after which the congregation responds, "Amen." Imagine that you are seated in your congregation of choice, listening to the following readings: "I will sing praise to your name, O Most High.... The enemies have vanished in everlasting ruins; their cities you have rooted out; the very memory of them has perished....

The LORD will swallow [up his enemies] in his wrath, and fire will consume them. [He] will destroy their offspring from the earth ... their children from ... humankind." (Psalms 9:2, 6, and 21:9-10) "[Thousands of angels] proclaimed with loud voices: 'Worthy is the Lamb who was slain, to receive power and wealth, wisdom and might, honor and glory and praise! I saw heaven wide open, and a white horse appeared; its rider's name was Faithful and True, for he is just in judgment and just in war.... He was robed in a garment dyed in blood, and he was called the Word of God. The armies of heaven followed him.... Out of his mouth came a sharp sword to smite the nations; for it is he who will rule them with a rod of iron, and tread the winepress of the fierce wrath of God the sovereign Lord." (Revelation 5:11-12 and 19:11, 13-15) "How many were the populations We [God] utterly destroyed because of their iniquities, setting up in their places other peoples. When they felt our punishment (coming) ... they (tried to) flee from it.... They said, 'Ah, woe to us! We were indeed wrongdoers! And that cry of theirs ceased not, till we made them as a field that is mown, as ashes silent and quenched." (Qur'an 21:11-15 Now if the reader were to end such passages with, "The Word of the Lord is Blessed," I hope that the congregation would not answer, "Amen," but rather, "I respectfully disagree," or "I don't think so." If such scripture is used to describe an enemy as your family friends and neighbor or perhaps to avoid causing unnecessary offense, the congregation might respond at that point with stone silence, then "argue nicely" after the service is over. Because these are not the words of a compassionate and just God towards, family, friends and neighbors. The God portrayed in those texts, is when GOD deals with the wickedness of those who denounce GOD and or deliberately mock GOD in the sins of life. Going against the commands of GOD that one would lead GOD to burn in anger over many who disregard His COMMANDMENTS. This is the "Spiritual Energy" at work!!!

CHAPTER I

WHO ARE YOU

The average volume of semen produced in a single release varies from 2 to 5 ml. The semen from a single release may contain between 40 million and 600 million sperm, depending on the volume of the release. Men with normal sperm counts can increase their chances of fathering a child through sexual relationships. A medical article shows that men with low sperm counts can increase their chances of fathering a child through extreme sexual relations. Ten to fifteen percent of couples are unable to have children. In more than 40% of marriages, a defect in male sperm is the cause. The normal release contains between 50 and 600 mil- lion sperm. Men who produce fewer than 50 million sperms often are infertile. Therefore, higher sperm counts increase a man's chances of fathering a child. A woman releases an egg once every 28 days and is fertile for only about 3 days a month. Twenty-four hours after she releases an egg, her body temperature rises one half a degrees. So a woman can take her early morning temperature and try to become pregnant on the morning of/ or before/ her body temperature rises. On the first try, normal men usually produce more than 600 million sperm. A second try 20 minutes later produces 120 million sperm. A third tries 6 hours later produces 10 million, and a fourth 24 hours later makes only 200,000. The latest research shows that men with low sperm counts do not reduce their sperm counts with consecutive releases. So, they could try to make love as often as possible when a woman releases an egg /or doctors can collect successive release and insert them together into the. The 200–600 million sperm normally found in a release, increases the chance that some will reach a mature egg, eventually with just one being able to enter and fertilize it. Evolution likely accounts for the high sperm count in a typical releases — a male who is able to produce more sperm obviously has a better likelihood of fertilizing a female than his competitors. In some species, this male may be the one with the largest testicles, which produce more sperm than smaller size. So, what happens to most of the released sperm on their journey to the egg? Well, as sperm swim through the vaginal canal and into the cervix, they hit a "fork in the road," so to speak. At this juncture, some sperm travel to one fallopian tube, while the rest move on to the other. However, only one fallopian tube has a fertile egg at a given time.

The sperm that do not reach an "impasse" surround the mature egg and compete with the other sperm in trying to penetrate it. If a woman's sexual and reproductive health is in good working condition, the first sperm to cross the finish line (enter the egg) succeeds in fertilizing it. "Helper" sperm can also be credited for easing fertilization by allowing this particular sperm access to and contact with the mature egg during its trip. With conception initiated, the now fertilized egg sets off some mechanisms, such as thickening of cervical mucus and hardening of its outer surface (zona pellucida), to block all other sperm from entering the egg.

Interestingly, some researchers have theorized that sperm have adapted to take on certain roles, other than for fertilization. For example, abnormal sperm that cannot fertilize may instead function to find and destroy or block competing sperm from other males that also may be making the rounds through

This hypothesis is not without much controversy. Alternatively, other researchers have argued that abnormal sperm are simply abnormal. Regardless, it's agreed that more research needs to be done on sperm structure and function before greater consensus can be made.

Studies show that one in every seven couples wishing to conceive is infertile. Earlier, it used to be assumed that the problem was solely due to disorders in the woman's reproductive system. However, it is now generally recognized in medical circles that 35-40% cases have male contributing factors. This is quite incredible considering an average, healthy male releases around 120 – 600 million sperm each time he releases. Reproduction should be easy for the male……but sometimes, things go a bit awry. Male infertility could be on account of congenital disorders or could be acquired at any time during his reproductive years and usually has to do with sperm abnormalities such as low sperm count, insufficient motility and abnormal morphology.

Here is the purpose within 600 million sperms traveling through woman's reproductive system and in this system there are two eggs within her fallopian tube to reach the uterus. Out of 600 Million Sperms fighting for position and only one single sperm is able to enter in one of the eggs.

Once entering that egg the most powerful process in "Eternal Life" take place called "The Germination Process," which through that entire process comes YOU! GOD chose you out of 600 Million Sperms to be the one to enter this world with powerful skills and abilities He place in you that His purpose and plan can be carried out, to make an impact here on this planet called "Earth". And so the question is do you really believe you were chosen out of 600 million sperms from your Daddy's loins, just to exist here on this powerful planet called earth.

SO YOU REALLY DON'T KNOW WHO YOU ARE?

THEN THERE'S THE COMMON WEALTH OF EARTH……

GENESIS 1:15 -17

Then the LORD God took the man and placed him in the Garden of Eden to cultivate and keep it.

And the LORD God commanded him, "You may eat freely from every tree of the garden, but you must not eat from the tree of the knowledge of good and evil; for in the day that you eat of it, you will surely die."

Here is the clear cut case of GOD establishing the meaning of "Common Wealth", to have access to all things, not ownership. GOD did not give Adam owner ship of the "Garden Of Eden" but simple access to the entire vast Garden Of Eden, stating in his word...you may eat freely from any tree in the garden, but not from the tree of good and evil. This is the principle of a common wealth society, such as the state of Virginia and Pennsylvania in the exercise of their imposed tax system of all places and things within these states.

It is a principle reason why these states thrive as an economically sound society within the United States. Simply by standing with the very principles of The Kingdom Of GODs common wealth economy which is access, not ownership. GOD never intended for man to own earth. So Find Yourself!!

FIND YOURSELF

What is a Kingdom?

1.) A kingdom is the sovereign ruler ship and governing influence of a king over its territory impacting it with his will, intent and purpose producing a community of citizens expressing a culture reflecting the nature and lifestyle of the king. Luke 17:20 The Kingdom of GOD does not come with your careful observation 21.) nor will people say, here it is or there it is, because the kingdom of GOD is within you.

2.)The Kingdom of God is the Heavenly sovereign ruler ship and governing influence of a King (Jesus Christ) over the earth and everything in it…in other words under a kingdom you become just like the king. Isaiah 9:6-7 "For to us a child is born, to us a son is given, and the government will be on his shoulders. And he will be called Wonderful Counselor, Mighty God, Everlasting Father, and Prince of Peace. Of the increase of his government and peace there will be no end

What makes a kingdom? And, Why a government?

A Kingdom is:

   1.) Land

   2.) Language

   3.) Laws

   4.) Symbols - such as a crown and not a cross

   5.) Constitution

   6.) Moral Code-meaning a standard of living

   7.) Shared Values

   8.) Custom - meaning giving an offering

   9.) Social - the norm - certainty

   10.) Culture -The way of life

Every nation seeks after good Government. What is Government? Government is the mandate of the nations. Government is the source of:

1.) INFLUENCE ~ Control = Impact

2.) PHILOSOPHY ~ Belief = Policy

3.) LAW ~ Standard = Lifestyle, how one lives in the land

4.) VALUE ~ Establish Society Worth = Human Self Worth

5.) Moral Standards ~ Social Behavior = Community Activity

6.) CULTURE ~ Lifestyle = Morality

7.) COMMUNITY ~ Corporate Expression = Language

8.) SOCIETY ~ Social Relations = Habits

9.) NATION ~ Community = Controlled Environments

It is the nature of the kingdom because the glory of the kingdom is in its territory….in other words the more territory a king has the greater his glory. This is called colonization which is expansion meaning a kingdom is extending its influence to a foreign territory. Mankind was created by God for the purpose of extending its territory to earth. Isaiah 45:18 "he who created the earth he is God; he who fashioned and made the earth, he founded it; he did not create it to empty, but formed it to be inhabited When a kingdom colonizes a territory ….the territory is totally provided for by the kingdom….. however that territory must remain depended on the kingdom in order to get its needs met. See religion doesn't do that… religion makes you beg God…religion makes you depended on people, it makes you offer all these sacrifices to God that rejects it. Know this, in a kingdom the wealth is common it's called common wealth.

We cannot wonder, therefore, at finding Adam subject to a probation; and even if he had remained innocent we have no right to suppose that his posterity would always have withstood temptation, or that the world would not finally have become in the condition as it is now. But the Kingdom Common Wealth conditions of Adam was different in the Garden of Eden and had unlimited freedom, except in one small particular area in the middle of the Garden, and no promptings of his own nature urged him to take delight in disobedience and sin. But if Adam was free from passion, on the other hand and his conscience was under-developed, even if it could be said to exist at all in one who did not know the difference between good and evil, there was no struggle between passion and conscience, man had not then learned to choose between opposing ends and purposes, as he has now. Nevertheless, Adam was an intellectual being. He had a deep knowledge of nature by that he called the animals after their kind. In Genesis..2:23 he calls his wife *Ishah,* and himself *Ish.* Now, this name signifies a *being,* and in so calling himself Adam seems to claim for man that he is the one creature upon earth conscious of his own existence. And when Eve appears he simply adds a feminine termination to the name, recognizing her thereby as the female counterpart of himself; but in so doing he shows a mastery of language, and the power of inflecting words according to the rules of grammar. There is proof, after the fall, of even increased insight into the nature of things; for in the name Eve, *life,* Adam plainly recognized in her difference of sex the Divinely-appointed means for the maintenance of human life upon earth. But man now, to balance the corruption of his nature, has, in addition to intellect, the help of conscience, of increased knowledge and experience of the effects of sin, and of largely developed reason. A difficult process of intended economics, such as is the lot of mankind now, would apparently have been beyond the power of Adam to sustain; whereas, had he not been tempted from without, he might easily, with his passions as yet unstirred, and most of his intellectual gifts still dormant, have endured the simple trial to which he was subjected. But temptation was permitted, and as we know now Adam fell.

It would be easy to lose ourselves in reasoning upon the possibilities involved in Adam's days, but there are points upon which there can be no doubt. If process is the normal law of our condition now, it would be just as right and equitable to make Adam subject to the process of GODs economic intentions for man. And alike for Adam then and for men now, the economic process of the Kingdom Common Wealth seems to be a necessary condition of the existence of humans being endowed with free will access to all the earth. The fall was not all a loss; Paul affirms this with reference to the gift of a Savior (Romans 5:17-19). And besides this, higher qualities are called into existence now than were possible in the case of one who had no experimental knowledge of evil. We may even say that in giving this command GOD was appealing to qualities still dormant in Adam; and this exercise of the Divine attribute of foreknowledge makes us sure that the Divine purpose was to develop these economic qualities: not necessarily, however, by the fall. For they would have been to some extent exercised by resisting temptation Adam, had he remained innocent, could nevertheless have attained to no higher economic state than such as was possible for a human being in a passionless state of existence. He would have attained to the perfection of innocence, of pure physical enjoyment, and of even large scientific knowledge; but his moral nature would have developed very slowly. He would have been a happy grown-up child, not a proved and perfected man. The sufferings of this fallen world are intense economically today (Romans 8:22), but the product in those who use their purpose right, will stand up higher than any product of Paradise could have been. The holiness attained to by Eloah (Mighty, or Powerful One). Adam, was of a different and higher kind than the most perfect innocence of a being who had been called to make no earnest struggle; for it was as the gold tried in the fire (<u>1Peter 1:7</u>). 1Peter 2:16,17 Let us never set up our own will against the Holy will of God. There was not only liberty(free will) allowed to man, complete access in taking the fruits of a vast Garden beyond the mind of man, but everlasting life made sure to him upon his obedience.

There was a trial appointed of his obedience. By transgression he would forfeit GOD's favor, and deserve his displeasure, with all its awful effects; so that he would become liable to pain, disease, death and destruction. Worse than that, he would lose the Holy Image of God, and all the comfort of his favor; and feel the torment of sinful passions, and the terror of his Maker's vengeance, which must endure for ever with his never dying soul. The forbidding to eat of the fruit of a particular tree was wisely suited to the state of our first parents. In their state of innocence, and separated from any others, what opportunity or what temptation had they to break any of the ten commandments? These event proves that the whole human race were under trial for the fall of Adam. To argue against these things is to strive against stubborn facts, as well as Divine revelation; for man has become sinful, and shows by his first actions, and his conduct ever afterwards, that he is ready to do evil. He is under the Divine displeasure, exposed to sufferings and death. The Scriptures always speak of man as of this sinful character, and in this miserable state; and these things are true of men in all ages, and of all nations. And the Lord God commanded the man, saying. - This is a the first principles(first law) of our intellectual and moral philosophy. The command here given in words brings into activity the intellectual nature of man. First, the power of understanding language is called forth. The command here addressed to him by his Maker is totally different from the blessings addressed to the animals in the preceding chapter. It was not necessary that these blessings should be understood in order to be carried into effect, inasmuch as He who pronounced them gave the instincts and powers requisite to their accomplishment. But this command addressed to man in words must be understood in order to be obeyed. The capacity for understanding language, then, was originally lodged in the constitution of man, and only required to be called out by the articulate voice of God. Still there is something wonderful here, something beyond the present grasp and promptitude of human apprehension.

If we except the blessing, which may not have been heard, or may not have been uttered before this command, these words were absolutely the first that were heard by man. The significance of the sentences they formed must have been at the same time conveyed to man by immediate divine teaching. How the lesson was taught in an instant of time can only be explained in an economic sense, though we have a distant understanding of it in an infant learning process. This process, indeed, goes over a space of time, but still there is an instant in which the first conception of a economy is formed, the first word is apprehended, the first sentence is understood. In that instant the knowledge of economic language is virtually attained. With man, created at once in his full undeveloped powers, and still unaffected by any tainted moral, this came with principle spoken laws to his ear and to his soul by his Maker's impressive voice, and the first economic lesson of language was at once thoroughly taught and learned. Man is now master of the theory of speech; the conception of a sign has been conveyed into his mind. This is the passive lesson of economics: the practice, the active lesson, had speedily followed. The primary and fundamental principles of man's intellectual nature has been developed in a Kingdom common wealth constitution. The understanding of the Kingdom common wealth necessarily implies the knowledge of the world's financial system. The objective is represented here by the "trees of the garden." The subjective comes before his mind in the pronoun "You." The physical constitution of man appears in the process of "eating." The moral part of his nature comes out in the significance of the words "may" and "shall not." The distinction of merit in actions and things is expressed in the epithets "good and evil." The notion of reward is conveyed in the terms "life" and "death." And, lastly, the presence and authority of "the Lord God" is implied in the very nature of a command. Here is at least the opening of a wide field of meaning of the Kingdom Common Wealth, which is "Access".

Man, indeed, must bear the image of God in perceptive powers. But as with the power, so with heedful eyes the loftiest as well as the lowest in a glance of intelligence begins the process of the mind with the reality of the world around, and the enlargement of human knowledge in a matter of time without end. How rapidly the process of human understanding would go on in the dawn of man's intellectual activity, how many flashes of intelligence would be compressed into a few moments of his first consciousness, only history can tell. But man can readily believe that he would soon be able to form a just yet a economic view of the things which are presented to his mind in this brief command. The moral nature of man's is constantly called into play with God's mode of teaching in His command. This is required in order to bring forth into consciousness the moral obligation which was laid in the original constitution of man's being. A command implies a superior, whose right it is to command, and an inferior, whose duty it is to obey. The only ultimate and absolute ground of supremacy is creating, and of inferiority, being created. The Creator is the only proper and entire owner; and, within legitimate bounds, the owner has the right to do what he will with his own. The laying on of this command, therefore, brings man to the recognition of his dependence for being and for the character of that being on his Maker. From the knowledge of the fundamental relation of the created to the Creator springs an immediate sense of the obligation he is under to render strict obedience to the Author of his being. This is, therefore, man's first lesson in morals. It calls up in his soul the sense of duty, of right, of responsibility. These feelings could not have been directed to the moral nature laid in the soul, and only waited for the first command to awaken it into consciousness. This economic lesson, however, is only the principle effect of the command, and not the primary ground of GODs plan. The special mandate here is absolutely essential to the Kingdom common wealth adjustment of things in this new stage of creation. To the behest of the Creator, the only accessible rights to all the "Garden of Eden" lay in man himself.

In the great economic system of things, through the wonderful wisdom of GOD, the use of this common wealth system was to the needful well-being, the development, and purpose of man. Nevertheless, no one has a shadow of right in the original nature of things to the use of their own free will. And when a moral agent comes upon the stage of being, in order to mark out the sphere of his legitimate action, an explicit declaration of the rights over other created beings granted and reserved must be made. The very issue of the command proclaims man's original right of property to be, not inherent, but derived. As might be expected in these circumstances, the command has two clauses, - a permissive and a prohibitive. "Of every tree of the garden you may freely eat." This displays in conscious terms the benignity of the Creator. "But of the tree of the knowledge of good and evil you shall not eat." This signalizes the absolute ownership of the Creator over all the trees, and over man himself. One tree only is withheld, which, whatever were its qualities, was at all events not necessary to the well-being of man. All the others that were likely for sight and good for food, including the tree of life, are made over to him by complete access. In this original provision for the vested rights of man in creation, it can be acknowledge with gratitude and humility the generous and considerate bounty of the Creator. This is not more bestowment of all the other trees than in the withholding of the one, to the process of which was the introduction of evil to mankind. The prohibited part of this enactment is not a matter of indifference, as is sometimes imagined, but indispensable to the nature of a command, and, in particular, of a permissive act or declaration of granted rights. Every command has a negative part, expressed or implied, without which it would be no command at all. The command, "Go work today in my vineyard," implies you shall not do anything else; otherwise the son who works not obeys as well as the son who works. The present address of God to Adam, without the exceptive clause, would be a mere license, and not a command.

But with the exceptive clause it is a command, and tantamount in meaning to the following positive injunction: You may eat of these trees only. An edict of license with a restrictive clause is the mildest form of command that could have been imposed for the trial of human obedience. Some may have thought that it would have been better for man if there had been no tree of the knowledge of good and evil.

But second thoughts will correct this rash and wrong conclusion. First. This tree have had other purposes to serve in the economy of things of which we are now aware; and, it has been absent without detriment to the general good. Second. But without any supposition at all, the tree was with no evil whatever to man in itself. It was in the first instance the instrument of great good, of the most precious kind, to him. It served the purpose of calling up into view the Kingdom common wealth system of things out of the depths of man's nature the notion of moral obligation, with all the kindred notions of the inherent authority of the Creator and the innate subordination of himself, the created, of the aboriginal right of the Creator

alone in all the creatures, and the utter absence of any right in himself to any other creature whatsoever. The command concerning this tree thus set his moral convictions going, and awakened in him the new and pleasing consciousness that he was a moral being, and not a mere dry bones of the valley or brute of the field. This is the first thing this tree did for man, establish "The Kingdom Common wealth System" and we shall find it would have done a still better thing for him if he had only made a proper use of it. The absence of this tree would not at all have secured Adam from the possibility or the consequence of disobedience. Any grant to him whatsoever must have been made "with the reserve," implicit or explicit, of the rights of all others. "The thing reserved" must in equity have been made known to him. In that present course of things it must have come in his way, and his trial would have been inevitable, and therefore his fall possible. Now, the forbidden tree is merely the thing reserved.

Besides, even if man had been introduced into a sphere of existence where no reserved tree or other thing could ever have come within the range of his observation, and so no outward act of disobedience could have been perpetrated, still, as a being of moral susceptibility, he must come to the acknowledgment, express or implied, of the rights of the heavenly crown, before a mutual good understanding could have been established between him and The Almighty GOD. Thus, we perceive that even in the impossible Utopia of metaphysical abstraction there is a virtual forbidden tree which forms the test of a man's moral relation to his Creator. Now, if the reserve be necessary, and therefore the test of obedience inevitable, to a moral being, it only remains to inquire whether the test employed be suitable and seasonable.

What is here made the matter of reserve, and so the test of obedience, is so far from being trivial or out of place, as has been imagined, that it is the proper and the only object immediately available for these purposes. The immediate need of man is food. The kind of food primarily designed for him is the fruit of trees. Grain, the secondary kind of vegetable diet, is the product of the farm rather than of the garden, and therefore does not now come into use. As the law must be laid down before man proceeds to an act of appropriation, the matter of reserve and consequent test of obedience is the fruit of a tree. Only by this can man at present learn the lessons of the Kingdom common wealth. To devise any other means, not arising from the actual state of things in which man was placed, would have been a worst state of mind. The immediate sphere of obedience lies in the circumstances in which man actually stands. These afforded no occasion for any other command than what is given. Adam had no father, or mother, or neighbor, male or female, and therefore the second table of the law could not apply. But he had a relation to his Maker, and legislation on this could not be postponed. The command assumes the kindest, most intelligible, and convenient form for the infantile mind of primeval man. We now must understand why this tree is called the tree of the knowledge of good and evil. The prohibition of this tree brings man to the knowledge of good and evil.

The products of creative power were all very good Genesis 1:31. Even this tree itself is good, and productivity of unspeakable good in the first instance to man. The discernment of merit comes up in his mind by this tree. Obedience to the command of God not to partake of this tree is a moral good. Disobedience to God by partaking of it is a moral evil.

When we have formed an idea of quality discipline decision making processes, we have at the same time an idea of its truths. By the command concerning this tree man became possessed of the conceptions of good and evil, and so, theoretically, acquainted with their nature. This was that first lesson in morals of which we now live. It is quite evident that this knowledge could not be any physical effect of the tree, seeing its fruit was forbidden. It is obvious also that evil is as yet highly known in this fair world only as the negative of good. Hence, the tree is the tree of the knowledge of good and evil, because by the command concerning it man comes to this knowledge.

"In the day of you eat of it, you shall surely die." The divine command is accompanied with its awful sanction - death. The man could not at this time have any practical knowledge of the physical dissolution called death. We must, therefore, suppose either that God made him preternaturally acquainted with it, or that he conveyed to him the knowledge of it simply as the negation of life. The latter hypothesis is to be preferred, for several reasons. It is the more economical mode of instruction. Such knowledge may be imparted to man without anticipating experience. He was already conscious of life as a pure blessing. He was therefore capable of forming an idea of its loss. And death in the physical sense of the cessation of animal life and the disorganization of the body, he would come to understand in due time by experience. 2nd), death in reference to man is regarded in Scripture much more as the privation of life in the sense of a state of favor with God and consequent happiness than as the mere cessation of animal life Genesis 28:13; Exodus 3:6; Matthew 22:32. 3rd), the presence and privilege of the tree of life would enable man to see how easily he could be deprived of life, especially when man began to drink in its life-sustaining juices and feel the flow of vitality rushing through his veins and refreshing his whole physical nature. Take away this tree, and with all the other resources of nature he cannot but eventually droop and die. Man would thus regard his exclusion from the tree of life as the earnest of the sentence which would come to its fullness, when the animal frame would at length sink down under the wear and tear of life like the beasts that perish. Then would ensue to the dead but perpetually existing soul of man the total privation of all the sweets of life, and the experience of all the ills of penal death. GOD put the man into the garden of Eden to dress it—not only to give him a pleasant economically sound life, but to place him in his process of the Kingdom Common Wealth of Life, and as the title of this garden, the garden of the Lord (Gen 13:10; Eze 28:13), indicates, it was in fact a temple in which he worshipped God, and was daily employed in offering the sacrifices of thanksgiving and praise. God commanded the woman too, as appears both from the permission for eating herbs and fruits given to her, together with her husband, Genesis 1:28-29, and from Genesis 3:1-3, and from Eve's punishment, and that either immediately, or by Adam, whom God enjoined to inform her thereof. **You may freely eat;** without offence to me, or hurt to Yourself. The words in Hebrew have the form of a command, but are only a permission or indulgence, as 1 Corinthians 10:25-27. And the Lord God commanded the man,.... Over whom he had power and authority; and he had a right to command him what he pleased, being his Creator, benefactor, and preserver; and this is to be understood not of man only, but of the woman also, whose creation, though related afterwards, yet was before this grant access to eat of all the trees of the "The Kingdom Common Wealth Garden of Eden" but one, and the prohibition of the fruit of that; for that she was in being, and present at this time, seems manifest from Genesis 3:2. saying, of every tree of the garden you may freely eat: a very generous, vast, and liberal allowance this: or "in eating you may eat", which was giving full power, and leaving them without any doubt and uncertainty about their food; which they might freely take, and freely eat of, wherever they found it, or were inclined to, even of any, and every tree in the garden, excepting one as forbidden.

CHAPTER II

"WHY ARE YOU HERE"

Why Are You Here?

In the beginning, God made the heavens and the earth, day and night, and all the animals on our planet - for a purpose. However, did He create man as some kind of hobby? Have you ever wondered WHY you were born? Does our existence END at death? What is our ultimate destiny? Do we exist to rule the UNIVERSE? The culmination of all creation was to make us "Then God said, 'Let Us make man in Our image, according to Our likeness; let them have dominion over the fish of the sea, over the birds of the air, and over the cattle, over all the earth and over every creeping thing that creeps on the earth. Genesis 1:26. The Hebrew word for God is Elohim, which is a plural form, and for that reason, we find the One who is the Creator referring to "our" image. Amazingly, God consists of more than one being. As the Bible continues its revelation of these Beings, it shows them in a family relationship. Was Adam immortal? Mankind were created in the divine likeness (verse 27), yet physical. When Adam took his first breath, he became a living being. He did not become an immortal spirit on the same level as God, for Ezekiel 18:4 tells us: "Behold, all souls are Mine . . . The soul who sins shall die." (Ezekiel 18:4). The Hebrew word translated as "soul" is "nephesh" which is also used in reference to animals but translated as "creature" in Genesis 1:20, 21, and 24. How could God make man in his own image if he did not give him an immortal spirit? God made Adam to look like himself. He gave him a mind capable of reasoning, thinking, and even creating, although his intellectual powers, in comparison, are limited. Adam came from the dust, the basic element of the earth, which of itself is inorganic or without life. Our Maker had to breathe the breath of life into Adam to make him a fully functioning Being.

God put Adam and Eve in the Garden of Eden specially designed for them. There were two unique trees in that paradise, a tree of life, and a tree of the knowledge of good and evil (Genesis 2:9). Notice what the first humans were told: "And the Lord God commanded . . . 'Of every tree of the garden you may freely eat; but of the tree of the knowledge of good and evil you shall not eat, for in the day that you eat of it you shall surely die.' "(Genesis 2:16-17). The implication is that they could have eaten of the tree of life and lived eternally (1000 years). Instead, they chose the other tree and set in motion a world subject to the bondage of corruption, as Paul said in Romans 8:21.As soon as they ate the fruit, they felt different about themselves and their Maker. They were ashamed of their nakedness and wanted to hide from God. Their innocent, trusting relationship with God vanished. They had knowledge of good and evil, but it was not what they expected. Their ultimate punishment was death: ". . . 'For dust you are, and to dust you shall return.' "(Genesis 3:19). God cast Adam and Eve out of the Garden of Eden because of their disobedience and unbelief. They would now have to rest living from a world cursed with thorns and thistles. Humanity had started on the path to destruction. It did not take Adam's children very long to harness the elements to form iron and other metals. They made implements and constructed buildings. They developed a social structure. Left to their own devices, the children of Adam grew so depraved that God had to send a flood to cleanse the earth and start anew with the family of Noah. Because he has allowed us to choose (Our will) our own course, many people do not believe that a divine Creator exists. It is common to hear questions like, "If there is a God, why does He allow crime, war, and disease? If He is truly powerful, why does He not stop these evils? And why does he seem to HIDE Himself?"Many religions teach the separation of man from God due to "the fall." Our creation was perfect and complete; Satan manipulated the mind of Eve which led both Adam and Eve to disregard GODS command, causing a fall from grace.

Religion will tell you that God had to come up with some kind of plan to SALVAGE His creation a plan to repair the damage. They would have you believe that he has been in a contest with devil business since and that the contest continues to this very day. But the Bible says "I form the light and created darkness, I bring prosperity and create disaster; I the Lord, do all these things. Isaiah 45:7. It is important to note that God is in control of Good and Evil! So Satan was a part of GODs plan and purpose which was set before the foundation of the world the scriptures points out. We are GODS greatest achievement, through the human reproductive process He set in motion, God has created countless human beings (regardless of the census stating of 7 Billion people on earth). Moreover, it is His desire that every one of us become complete in His eyes. The Rapture will begin the process when mankind's nature transforms into our complete nature. It is vitally important that we understand how God redeems us. Our salvation is by grace through faith. Christians are His workmanship created in Christ Jesus to perform good works (Ephesians. 2:8-10). Many religions would have you believe that there are NO WORKS involved in following Christ. Many Religions teach a person need only accept Jesus to receive salvation. This is not what the Bible teaches! Jesus gave Himself for us:" . . . that He might redeem us from every lawless deed and purify for Himself His own special people, zealous for good works." (Titus. 2:14). The Christian's good works stand as a witness to unbelievers, who will remember them and glorify God in the day of visitation (1Peter 2:12). The plan of salvation will come when Jesus Christ returns to this earth. At that time, He will resurrect those who have died in faith (1 Thessalonians. 4:16-17, Daniel. 12:2-3) and will bring their reward with Him (Revelation. 22:12, Matthew. 16:27). Their reward will be according to their works. (1Cor.10:17). How does a person obtain salvation? What motivates him to want to produce good works and to remain faithful to the end? Before we can walk with God, we must change our way of thinking. To most people, that means remorse(being sorry).

The Christian Bible, however, has written much more. In preparing the way for Jesus the one they call the Messiah, John the Baptist taught the necessity of receiving baptism and bringing forth evidence of repentance (Matthew. 3:8-11). Jesus preached repentance."From that time Jesus began to preach and to say, 'Repent, for the kingdom of heaven is at hand.' "(Matthew. 4:17). Peter cried to the multitudes in Jerusalem gathered to observe the day of Pentecost:"Then Peter said to them, 'Repent, and let every one of you be baptized in the name of Jesus Christ for the remission of sins; and you shall receive the gift of the Holy Spirit. (Acts. 2:38). The first step in salvation is a change of mind, recognition that your ways are not those of the Father and that thru the act of sin have separated you from GOD."For godly sorrow produces repentance leading to salvation, not to be regretted; but the sorrow of the world produces death. "(2 Corinthians 7:10). The apostle Paul recognized that he had been a blasphemer, a persecutor, and a destroyer. He wrote to his friend Timothy and said: "And I thank Christ Jesus our Lord who has enabled me, because He counted me faithful, putting me into the ministry, although I was formerly a blasphemer, a persecutor . . . but I obtained mercy because I did it ignorantly in unbelief . . .

This is a faithful saying and worthy of all acceptances, that Christ Jesus came into the world to save sinners, of whom I am chief." (1Timothy.1:12-13, 15). Despite the sins we did and would commit, God was willing for Paul and all other human beings to be saved and to come to the knowledge of the truth (1Timothy 2:4). He is willing to forgive if we confess our sins and change our lives according to His commandments (Rom.10:9).Once a person has fully repented and been baptized, the Holy Spirit renews his mind (Ephesians. 4:23-24). The Christian becomes a NEW CREATION (2 Corinthians 5:17), who must no longer conform to the values of a world led by the devil. The Citizen of the Kingdom of Heaven must learn to live by God's Word, on Earth:"All Scripture is given by inspiration of God, and is profitable for doctrine, for reproof, for correction, for instruction in righteousness . . ."

(2 Timothy 3:16-17). The Bible corrects us and helps us to discern our innermost feelings as they compare to God's way of life. Man has perverted the word of God, polluted his mind, and let his body degenerate. He has failed to train or has wrongly taught his children. He feels resentment and envy - even hatred - toward his neighbor. He tries to get more out of life than he puts in. Yes, why are we special? What potential does GOD see in us? "You have made him a little lower than the angels; you have crowned him with glory and honor, and set him over the works of your hands." Not all things are under our feet just yet. It took Jesus Christ, who as God came in the form of a human, to bring all things into subjection and to taste death for everyone:"For it was fitting for Him, for who are all things and by who are all things, in bringing many sons to glory, to make the captain of their salvation perfect through sufferings."(Hebrews 2:10).

The truly converted Citizen of the Kingdom of Heaven becomes a child of God -- a member of a Family first known to man as Elohim. In the beginning, the Family consisted of only two Supreme Beings. Now, it composed of many sons and daughters who will receive eternal life. Jesus is the firstborn of MANY BRETHREN (Romans. 8:29)."Beloved, now we are children of God we shall be like Him, for we shall see Him as He is." (1 John. 3:2).Why did God create us? The purpose of man rests in the plan of salvation and his goal to make man after His own Image. God has reproducing Himself through men and women that He calls a Citizen of the Kingdom of Heaven. When such a person, through baptism, receives the gift of the Holy Spirit, he or she becomes a spiritual son or daughter, though not yet spiritually born again until the confession of (Rom. 10:9). Through Biblical studies day and night, daily prayer, and the experiences and trials of life, the Christian grows spiritually. His human, self-centered nature is reformed and shaped into godly character. Then, at the time of the resurrection, the Christian transforms from mortal to immortal. He is born again. Only this time, he is born into the divine Family, and not into a human family.

As he was once born in the image of his human parents, his spiritual birth is the image of GOD. The resurrected Christian will exist and be part of his growing family! This is the wonderful truth why God made us in the first place! May God bless you and give you insight into the meaning and importance of the greatest commandment ever spoken: "Love the Lord your God with all your heart and with all your soul and with all your strength!" (Mark. 12:30)

CHAPTER III

YOUR PURPOSE

Until the restoration of earth and God's reconstitution of the heavenly lights, Lucifer, the "light-bearer" and his followers had found themselves in the dark, awaiting their fate. Satan's coup d'état had ended a dismal failure, and his nefarious experimentations on earth, the original Eden, had been summarily terminated by a divine intervention that left not only the earth but the surrounding universe as well buried in deep darkness. We know from the testimony of scripture that a trial followed in which God condemned Satan and his fallen angels for their rejection of His authority and for their rebellion:

Behold, He does not place [unreserved] trust in His servants, but charges [even] His angels with error. Job 4:18

Then He will say to those on His left, "Away from Me, you accursed ones, into the eternal fire [already] prepared for the devil and his angels.

Matthew 25:41

Concerning judgment, because the ruler of this world has been condemned. John 16:11   Satan's case (and that of his followers) has thus already been adjudicated and his ultimate fate pronounced. By the time he and his fallen angels are cast down to the earth during the Great Tribulation (Rev.12:7-9), he will be well aware of the fact that he has "but little time left" (Rev.12:12).

At the conclusion of mankind, but not until that point has been reached at the end of the millennial rule of GOD, Devil Business will face the execution of his sentence (Rev.20:10; Is.24:21-22), a verdict adjudged before human history began. The question may well be posed, "why the delay in judgment? Why did God not simply plunge the devil and his minions into the fires of hell immediately after their just condemnation?" The answer to all such questions is intimately bound up with God's creation of another species of sentient, morally responsible creatures, namely, Man. So it is that to the purpose, creation and fall of mankind that we must now turn.

Though already under sentence of death for his unrepentant attempt to overthrow God's rule over the universe (Job 4:18; Matt.25:41; Jn.16:11), Satan still retains his freedom of action. We find him spying on our first parents in the garden (Gen.3), appearing before the Lord to slander our brethren (Job 1&2; Zech.3; Rev.12:10), and prowling the earth in search of believers whose defenses are down (1Pet.5:8). The reason for the devil's intense interest in mankind is similar to the reason for our creation in the first place (and to the reason for the delay in carrying out the sentence of death under which he stands as well): Man is meant as a response to Satan's rebellion, a living refutation of the devil's slanderous lies against the character of God. God has created mankind 1) to demonstrate to all angelic kind His ability to reconcile His creatures to Himself, and 2) to actually replace all that was lost through the devil's defection. Man created to demonstrate God's righteousness in acting mercifully: Although every aspect of God's perfect character is visible in His gracious dealings with the human race, the demonstration of His righteousness toward us in salvation most directly answers Satan's slanders regarding God's ability to provide reconciliation. It will be remembered that part of the devil's appeal to his potential followers rested on his assurance that God would be unable to effect any reconciliation between Himself and His rebellious creatures. Devil reasoned that God's righteousness would stand in the way of His mercy and thus make forgiveness impossible. God would thus be "put in a box", unable to act in mercy without compromise, unable to execute punishment without permanently marring His creation in an irreversible way. No matter how much He might dislike it, God would be forced to tolerate Satan's usurpation of power. And though it would not have formed part of his public pitch, the devil was no doubt also working on the "safety in numbers" principle, reckoning that while God might choose to chastise one rebel, removing the vast multitude of angels whom Satan had been able to recruit would create an irreparable rift in the fabric of the universe.   But the devil's logic failed to take into account the ineffable love of God, and was oblivious to the idea that our God is a God of such grace that He would even sacrifice His most beloved possession, His Son, Jesus Christ, on our behalf.

Devil spoke correctly about the righteousness of God preventing His mercy from arbitrarily forgiving sin in any form, but what the devil did not count on was God's willingness to pay for sin Himself through the sacrifice of His Son, so that we might justly be accounted righteous in His eyes (2Cor.5:21):

For I am not ashamed of the gospel, because it is the power whereby God may save everyone who believes (whether the Jew first, or the Greek). Because in it the righteousness of God is revealed from faith to faith, as it is written, "[it is he who is] righteous on account of his faith [who] shall live".

Romans 1:16-17

We are saved by faith in the Person and work of the One who died in our place and paid the price of sin for us, our Lord and Savior Jesus Christ. Because Jesus paid the price, God can forgive our sin, not arbitrarily, but justly, since it has been paid for in full in the most precious coin. God is therefore not only merciful to forgive us and welcome us into His family when we believe in Jesus, He is also just in justifying us, righteous in proclaiming us righteous, "not from works of righteousness which we have done" (Tit.3:5), but from our acceptance of the work of the One who died for us. Angels being angels, any decision to rebel against God would be final. Possessed as they are of perceptive abilities that far exceed our material limitations, it can be truly said of them that "they knew what they were getting into" (at least as far as creatures can know). Reconciliation of fallen angels to a merciful God was therefore never a likely possibility – because they would not have it, not because God could not or would not do it. The truth of this last point He has proven irrefutably by the loving sacrifice of His only Son on mankind's behalf, paying a price so steep we can only dimly comprehend it. If the devil and his angels had been of a mind to receive such an incomparable gesture of sacrifice and mercy, God would have generously provided it. By giving up His Son to the cross, God has demonstrated beyond any shadow of a doubt both His willingness and His ability to rescue His creatures, for He has in fact done so for us, even though it meant paying the price His righteousness demanded with the blood of His own Son.

Thus human history is on the one hand a demonstration to angelic kind (elect as well as fallen) of God's mercy and His ability to act justly in providing that mercy (albeit at tremendous cost to Himself). We human beings are actually experiencing God's love and mercy as He provides for us here in the world despite the devil's opposition. To the angels, however, we are a demonstration of that love and mercy, made effective through the sacrifice of Jesus Christ and our faith in Him. Being spirits and so not subject to the material limits that so try our human hearts of flesh, they must learn by observation, and observe us they do in great earnestness (Job 1&2; Matt.18:10; Lk.15:10; 1Cor.4:9; 11:10; 1Pet.1:12). That this demonstration will have been one of over seven thousand years' duration (when human history shall have finally run its course) is merely further proof of the graciousness and long-suffering of God (Is.30:18; Rom.2:4; 2Pet.3:9; 3:15). Through the long course of this demonstration (which is our collective human experience), the elect angels will have come to know God and His perfect character better than ever before, while the fallen angels will see their leader's every blasphemous accusation refuted and destroyed in voluminous detail. And when all is said and done, God's righteousness will have been affirmed as beyond reproach, proved beyond a shadow of a doubt in the merciful salvation of believing mankind. Man created to replace Satan and his angels: The creation of Man following the Genesis Gap judgment is a clear indication that the two events are intimately related. For God to create a new species of creature, possessing along with the angels both spirituality and free will, and then to deposit them on the very scene of Satan's rebellious activity was no subtle indication that at least one of God's purposes for mankind would be the replacement of the devil and his death demons. This must have been abundantly and immediately clear to Satan. For here was a new moral creature who (left to his own devices) might just do what he and his would not: obey God's will without rebelling against Him. As the requisite population was reached through procreation, Satan and company could be removed. Wholeness and completeness having thus been restored and Judgment, after all, had already been pronounced (Job 4:18; Matt.25:41; Jn.16:11). What could remain except for a one-for-one replacement of fallen angels with human beings, once our numbers became sufficient?

With judgment set, execution of God's sentence against the devil would be inevitable if not immediate (Rev.20:10): And it will come to pass on that day (the "day of the Lord"), that the Lord will punish the host of heaven above (the devil and his angels), and the kings of the earth below (those who have opposed His Christ), and they will be gathered together, bound in a dungeon, jailed and imprisoned. And after many days they will be punished. Isaiah 24:21-22 Therefore, with the creation of Man, a creature capable of procreation unlike the angels, the de facto removal of the only remaining, tangible barrier to Satan's execution was only a matter of time. The principle of God's desire to retrieve what is lost and replace what is missing is clearly seen in scripture in the parable of the lost sheep (Matt.18:12-14; Lk.15:4-10), the law of levirate marriage (Deut.25:5-6), and, of course, in His longing for all mankind to accept the gift of Jesus Christ and   return to Him (Ezek.18:23; Matt.18:14; Jn.12:47; 2Pet.3:9): [God] who wants all men to be saved and come to accept the truth. 1st Timothy 2:4 There is ample evidence to suggest that elect mankind is, in effect, replacing fallen angelic kind in God's universal order (Lk.10:17-20; 1Cor.6:3; Rev.20:4). The principle is most clearly seen in the God-Man's replacement of the original covering cherub: Lucifer (the "light bearer") replaced by the Morning Star, Jesus Christ (Is.14:12 with 2Pet.1:19; Rev.2:28; 22:16). Thus it is only fitting that the followers of the Morning Star should   replace Lucifer's followers. In this way the wholeness and integrity of the creation will be restored, while everything that was lost will be replaced with something even better: willing worshipers of God in union with His Son, the God-Man, so that ultimately "God may be all in all" (1Cor.15:28). Satan's motives for precipitating the fall of Man are therefore clear. Unwilling to repent, neither could he afford to accept the new threat the status quo entailed. Man created for the glory of God: The replacement of Satan and his followers with willing worshipers, and the ample demonstration of God's love and righteousness through the sacrifice of His Son to save these sinful human beings abundantly redound to the great glory of God. After watching the events of human history unfold, the elect angels (and, in fact, all creatures) are moved to praise and glorify the Lord Almighty for His matchless grace (cf. Ps.148-150): To Him who sits on the throne and to the Lamb, be praise and honor and glory and power forever and ever! Revelation 5:13 NIV.   It is for God's praise, for God's glory, that we have been created (Is.60:21; Jn.17:10; 21:19; Rom.9:23).

By making us and by saving us through Christ, God shows His love and exposes the devil's lies. In us, in what He has done for us, the glory of God shines forth, and those who love Him cannot help but praise Him:

Having foreordained us in [His] love for adoption to Himself through Jesus Christ according to the good pleasure of His will, for the purpose of producing praise for the glory of His grace which He has graciously bestowed on us in the Beloved [One]. Ephesians 1:5-6

In whom we also have an inheritance, having been ordained according to the design of Him who is working everything out according to the desire of His will, that we who have previously placed our hope in Christ might serve the purpose of generating praise for His glory. Ephesians 1:11-12

Everyone who is called by my Name, for My glory I have created him, I have formed him, indeed, I have made him. Isaiah 43:7

As the passages above indicate, only regenerate human beings (i.e., believers in Christ) form the echelon of replacement for fallen angelic kind. Human beings who choose to reject God's gracious gift of Jesus Christ will share the fate of the devil and his followers in the lake of fire (Rev.20:11-15). This too is a part of the demonstration of the righteousness of God, and also redounds to His great glory. Not only will the entire universe witness His gracious provision of mercy towards all who turn to Him, but all who oppose His will, Satan and all rebels, be they angels or men, will be crushed materially (in judgment) as well as spiritually (through the demonstration of human history; Ps.76:10). And everyone, whether rebellious or regenerate, will eventually acknowledge the majesty, the righteousness, the glory of God:

 By Myself I have sworn. From my mouth a righteous word has gone forth, which will not be revoked, that every knee will bow to Me, and to Me every tongue will swear. And so they will acknowledge Me: "Only in the Lord are righteousness and might." Before Him will come all who raged against Him and they will be put to shame. Isaiah 45:23-24

It is in the nature of God not to let a lie stand, but instead to expose all lies to the blinding light of the truth. Human history constitutes, in effect, the "last judgment" of fallen angelic kind, a vivid, living demonstration of their error and utter sinfulness in the course of which "every mouth will be stopped" (every excuse destroyed: Rom.3:19; Ps.107:42; Mic.7:16) and at the end of which every knee will bow and tongue declare the glory of God and the grace of God in the gift of His Son our Lord Jesus Christ (Rom.14:11; Phil.2:10-11).

God has a beautiful plan for womanhood that will bring order and fulfillment if it is followed in obedience. God's plan is that one man and one woman, of equal standing before Him but of different roles, should be bonded together as one. In His wisdom and grace He specifically created each for his or her role. At creation, God caused a deep sleep to fall on Adam, and from him God took a rib and made a woman (Genesis 2:2 1). She was a direct gift from the hand of God, made from man and for man (1 Corinthians 11:9). "Male and female created he them", (Genesis 1:27) each different but made to complete and complement each other. Although the woman is considered the "weaker vessel" (1 Peter 3:7), this does not make her inferior. She was made with a purpose in life that only she could fill. To woman has been given one of the greatest privileges in the world, that of molding and nurturing a living soul. Her influence, especially in the realm of motherhood, affects her children's eternal destination. Even though Eve brought condemnation upon the world with her act of disobedience, God considered women worthy of a part in the plan of redemption (Genesis 3:15). "But when the fullness of the time was come, God sent forth his Son, made of a woman." (Galatians 4:4). He entrusted to her the bearing of and the caring for his own dear Son. The woman's role is not insignificant! A distinction between the sexes is taught throughout the Bible. Paul teaches if a man has long hair, it is a shame unto him, but if a woman has long hair, it is a glory to her (1 Corinthians 11:14, 15). "The woman shall not wear that which pertained unto a man, neither shall a man put on a woman's garment: for all that do so are abominations unto the Lord thy God" (Deuteronomy 22:5). Their roles are not to be interchangeable. In the Garden of Eden, God said, "It is not good that the man should be alone," and He made a help meet for him-a companion, someone to satisfy his needs

(Genesis 2:18). Proverbs 31:10-31 tells in detail what kind of help meet the woman is to be. The supportive role of the wife to the husband is very evident in this description of the ideal woman. She "will do him good and not evil." Because of her honesty, modesty and chastity, "her husband doth safely trust in her." By her efficiency and diligence she would look well to her household. The basis for her virtue is found in verse 30: "a woman that feared the Lord." This is a reverential fear that gives meaning and purpose to her life. Only as the Lord lives in her heart can she be the woman she was meant to be. To become a child of God she needs to repent, confess her sins and accept Christ through faith. With Christ she will be able to live a self-denied life. The Holy Spirit will give strength, courage, and direction to fulfill her duties. He will grace her life with humility, modesty, and with that inner "ornament of a meek and quiet spirit, which is in the sight of God of great price" (1 Peter 3:3, 4). Proper, modest dress adds to the hidden charm of a woman. She should never draw attention to her body by being overdressed or underdressed. To avoid confusion and establish order, someone needs to be the head and God has ordained that this should be the man (1 Corinthians 11:3). Marriage is to be a harmonious relationship similar to that of Christ and the Church. Christ is subject to God, man is subject to Christ, and woman is subject to man. Why would any woman rebel at her position in the framework of authority when even Christ, the Son, is subject to the Father? As the wife reverences her husband, she is obedient to the scripture (Ephesians 5:33), and her husband is then able to bear the responsibility that God has laid on his shoulders. The liberation movement has challenged God's blueprint for womanhood. Women are clamoring for freedom and fulfillment by asking for total equality. This puts them into a power struggle- into a competitive role instead of a complementary partnership. Their quest for freedom only leads them into bondage. Nevertheless, the selfishness and ungodliness of many men is without excuse. In this context some of women's frustrations can be understood. Ironically, the very thing that many women are rejecting is God's way of establishing the woman in a life that fully satisfies. If a women moves aggressively into the man's world and there seeks independence and equality, she loses her femininity that reserved, modest sweetness that men respect and God approves.

Fulfillment comes as she cultivates those gifts for which she was created. A woman's submission to her husband liberates her from a multitude of frustrating problems, and her submission to God's order frees her from guilt. Submission is a blessing, not a curse! The pattern of men taking the leadership and women following will bring a blessing to single women as well as married women, to daughters as well as wives. As an outward sign of this submission and her submission to Christ, the Christian woman is commanded to have her head covered for praying and prophesying (1 Corinthians 11:3-5). Man is subject to Christ and should therefore pray with his head uncovered. Woman is subject to man and should pray with her head covered. Wearing a head covering is recognition of this divine order. Love in marriage is to be pure and is given for pleasure as well as for propagation. Woman was uniquely created for the special task of bearing children, a creative fulfillment. God said, "Be fruitful and multiply" (Genesis 1:28). To purposely choose not to have children is sidestepping God's principle and forfeiting one of the most rewarding experiences in a woman's life. Woman's first duty is the making and keeping of her home. Many a modern woman chooses a career, hires a baby-sitter, and rushes her children through childhood so that she can be free to pursue her selfish interests. The Bible teaches that women are to be "keepers at home" (Titus 2:5). This means a women is to be there, loving her husband, teaching and enjoying her children, and applying the homemaking arts with joy in her heart. This mother is the heartbeat of the home. She helps lay the foundation of moral standards there. The warmth of her spirit quietly establishes security in the lives of little children-confidence, that in spite of their problems and fears, all will be right. Why would any woman trade this noble place for some dollars earned or for some coveted position? This Bible way is not just being old-fashioned; it is God's order. The women who wholeheartedly accept God's plan will be blessed. In certain instances, a woman's role extends beyond her home. Examples are given in both the Old and New Testaments of godly women who had responsibilities in God's kingdom. Also today there is a place for the Christian woman to serve within the Church. As she exercises her inborn attributes of love, gentleness, and compassion, she is a living example of that which becomes godliness. Older women are exhorted to teach the young women, "that the word of God be not blasphemed" (Titus 2:4,5).

Single Christian women, who do not have the cares of a home and a family, are able to fill a special place (1 Corinthians 7:34). There are definite guidelines for women's behavior in the Church. They are not to usurp authority over men. Paul instructs, "Let your women keep silence in the churches" (1 Corinthians 14:34,35; 1 Timothy 2:11-15). The order that God has planned for women excludes them from preaching. Faithful women find places for active participation in Christian service where they can humbly and consistently fellowship with other Christians. May each woman fill her role with the grace of God in her heart, live in submissive obedience to His will, and humbly give of herself in the daily practices of life. As each person fills his respective place in God's plan, there is beautiful harmony that emerges in the heart, the home, and the church.

THE WOMAN., When the wounded family comes in, the position of the woman steps in with her nurturing ways and means, the woman releases the love, the care, the compassion for the need of the family doing this time of difficulty, she express peace and joy to the kids who so yearn for her attention 24hrs a day. She carries the burden of comfort to every corner of the home that where ever Devil seeks to enter he will know that there is a battle ready suitable helper, woman and wife in that place with a love for her family and that she will not be compromised. The woman is the engineer of the home, as the Bibles says— in Prov. 14:1, "The wise woman builds her house, but with her own hands the foolish one tears hers down," But Prov. 9:1-6 says— " Wisdom has built her house; she has set up its seven pillars. She has prepared her meat and mixed her wine; she has also set her table. She has sent out her servants, and she calls from the highest point of the city, "Let all who are simple come to my house!" To those who have no sense she says," come; eat my food and drink of the wine I have mixed. Forsake your folly and live, and proceed in the way of understanding." The woman given the proper supplies from her husband sets the standards as to how the house runs or operates amongst the children, the husband sets the instructions out to the suitable helper which in intern dissect the instruction to the simplest form to the woman who then gathers all information transitioning it in her thinking, to her attitude, to her philosophy, to behavior and her action.

This gives the woman what she needs to build her house in to a home, fulfilling all needs to the every aspect of the "Husband and Child" so that her virtuous ways and means can exceed to the ways of the Old as Paul says. In— 1 Pet 3:1-6; GODLY LIVING in the same way, you wives, be submissive to your own husbands so that even if any of them are disobedient to the word, they may be won without a word by the behavior of their wives, as they observe your chaste and respectful behavior. Your adornment must not be merely external-braiding the hair, and wearing gold jewelry, or putting on dresses; but let it be the hidden person of the heart, with the imperishable quality of a gentle and quiet spirit, which is precious in the sight of God. For in this way in former times the holy woman also, who hoped in God, used to adorn themselves, being submissive to their own husbands; just as Sarah obeyed Abraham, calling him lord, and you have become her children if you do what is right without being frightened by any fear. What 1 Peter 3 is saying here is that this is the intended way of life for the woman to operate in; it is this mannerism that is acceptable with God and pleasing in his sight. Such differences or division hinders the prayers that the family seeks God to interfere in the families affairs; the woman is the heart of this threefold position of the female (suitable helper, woman and wife). But it is vitally important for the woman in her position to operate to the fullest, it is important to understand the husband's instructions for such instructions come from God as the husband is in line with the kingdom of God. The woman in her early rise is for the sake of instructions for the days family business, everything about the woman in her position is to transcend the family as to God the Father, in the name of Christ Jesus under the instructions of the Holy Spirit which is the instructions to the husbands which is instructions to the suitable helper, woman and wife to maintain the family. The greatest downfall of the family is division; division is to set apart; to separate, this is what we witness in the Garden of Eden with Adam and Eve. This division was so catastrophic to the human race, not God's purpose and plan but to man, leaving Adam and Eve under a great punishment that still stands today Gen. 3:1-23; (this is not a part of the curse) which redirected God original intention for the foundation of the family, altering temporarily, how the family should function. This fall occurred by way of the two standing together as one to eat of the fruit that made them like the trinity, as God said knowing good and evil.

This fall came by way of the suitable helper not the woman or the wife, "The wise woman builds her house, but with her own hands the foolish one tears hers down" (Prov. 14:1). Some of the world finest couples are divorced more than once and their families have been sacrificed for their job. This is hard enough for a man, but a woman has the authority of her husband and the authority she serves at work. Some would say that they have no problem in this area, but the rise in broken homes says much different. God intended the home to be the center of a women's world. This has been greatly attacked even in the days of the New Testament. In Titus 5:14 younger women were encouraged to marry, bear children, and guide the home so that they would not be attacked by the enemy. In Titus 2:5, older women were to encourage the younger women to love their husband and children and to be keepers of the home that the word of God might not be blasphemed. Why? Because they were not doing what Paul was trying to do, lead them back to God's design. It is when we as a society have rejected His plan that our plan will be in the opposite direction and will lead to disaster. One of these ways is when we justify women working outside of the home. 40 years ago most young women were graduating from high school, getting married and starting to raise a family. Today, however, our society is teaching them that they need a career to fall back on just in case their marriage does not last. What does the word of God say will happen when women work outside the home? The woman does not meet her highest potential, God designed the woman to be a helpmeet for her husband. Often you hear women say that they are tired of being identified as somebody's wife, and they have forgotten that they will be the only one in the world that will hold that title in the family? If a husband were to lose their job, the company would just hire another person to replace him and within a short time he would be forgotten. If the family loses the husband, they would be damaged and would never be their best in moving forward. The absence would be felt for years to come. The women of the house would then form an independent spirit, the scriptures tell us that for Husband to love your wives. . . . Wives submit to your husband (Col. 3:18-19). Not even men are to be independent. Nowhere in scripture does God want an independent person, but our adversary, the devil, promotes independence from God.

This is a damaging philosophy in marriages today. When a woman does not think she needs her husband or children, she will lose her love for them. This is one of the reasons why a growing number of couples do not have children. It reduces their independence and increases their so called freedom. She becomes financially unwise; This leads to a wakeup call to men that they should not to leave their wives, because of the hardships that they will bring upon them. Remember, she is your companion (best friend) and the wife of your covenant (Mal. 2:14). Many people lose sight on understanding how family should survive any level income, and or learn how to actually do better than most with two incomes. The women of the house would then form an independent spirit, the scriptures tell us that for Husband to love your wives. . . . Wives submit to your husband (Col. 3:18-19). Not even men are to be independent. Nowhere in scripture does God want an independent person, but our adversary, the devil, promotes independence from God. This is a damaging philosophy in marriages today. When a woman does not think she needs her husband or children, she will lose her love for them. This is one of the reasons why a growing number of couples do not have children. It reduces their independence and increases their so called freedom. She becomes financially unwise; This leads to a wakeup call to men that they should not to leave their wives, because of the hardships that they will bring upon them. Remember, she is your companion (best friend) and the wife of your covenant (Mal. 2:14). Many people lose sight on understanding how family should survive any level income, and or learn how to actually do better than most with two incomes. The Women's greatest asset is hindered, with time is our most valuable asset and the Bible tells us to number our days that we may apply our hearts to wisdom (Psalms 90:12). God has placed in every women the gifts and talents to teach and train her children, not the daycare system. Scripture teaches that when a child is left to himself, he will bring his mother to shame (Proverbs 29:15). The Hebrew word for left is translated Shalach which means to send away. When women send their children out from their God given responsibilities it will bring shame to her. Women cannot fulfill their responsibility unless their husbands establish a platform for them to do that. We, as a nation, have forgotten the influencing power women have over her children and what mighty things she can accomplish for her community and the Kingdom of God when she has a platform in the home.

Women can be tempted to transfer her affections away from their husbands. This is something that happens all over our nation: women having affairs with men in the work place. This is a major cause that lead up to an affair. As people work together, they talk and become friends. As problems develop at home, usually financial, discussions take place and soon she starts comparing the men at work to her husband. Even though an affair may never take place, she has misplaced some of her affections away from her husband and has damaged her marriage. Soon the husband realizes that she doesn't depend on him like she used to. Distrust and even jealousy raises its ugly head. When women get together and talk about their husband's it's usually in a negative outcome. They disgrace themselves, because they are degrading the one that they vowed to love, cherish and honor for the rest of their lives before GOD. This brings on an automatic punishment by way of adultery from the hand of GOD.

CHAPTER IV

THE IDENITY CRISIS

An identity crisis is a time in life when an individual begins to seriously quest for answers about the nature of his or her being and the search for an identity. Most persons go through periods of defiance against authority figures. Part of this "defining against" authority figures is identity crisis. Though kids may make extremely poor choices when they choose to defy parents, they are often participating in a deep exploration of self that will help them determine what they will do and who they will be as they enter adulthood. For parents, watching a child enter the identity crisis stage is often fearful and difficult, since deliberate disobedience to certain standards may be inherently risky. Kids can unfortunately wreck their futures if they push too far away from parental or societal law; they could end up addicted to drugs or parenting children of their own far before they're ready. Nevertheless, most children must make this fearful passage to find a unique identity. When they are in the midst of it, this may be called the moratorium stage. In this part choices are being evaluated and explored, and there might be high incidence of exploration or various ideas, interests, career, sexuality, and etc. Once through the crisis a person has what is called identity achievement. They have set their feet on a path and determined who they are and what they want to be. This isn't only about determining a potential career. Such a crisis can be about exploring sexual identity and deciding what ethics and values are most important. Some people end up on a path that determines their identity without exploration or introspection and this may be called a foreclosure state. Some social scientists feel that a foreclosure will precipitate an identity crisis at a later point, since little exploration about choice was made. Occasionally people who live in very restrictive environments have their choice made for them, and an identity is established without much choice or examination of other options. There are certain cultures that deeply encourage and facilitate an identity crisis. In Amish cultures, some communities encourages older teens to live in the outside world before determining whether they will remain a permanent part of the Amish community and be baptized. Similarly, some Roman Catholic communities now have changed confirmation to a later time, or encourage people to take time to consider whether they truly wish to be confirmed in the Catholic Church.

Allowing an identity to emerge before making such important decisions seems psychologically sound. As mentioned, the identity crisis is not redistricted to adolescence and the emergence into adulthood. It can occur at any time, and many people label the "Midlife Crisis" as a crisis of identity. Some people find their values, choice, or paths inappropriate after major life changes like a divorce. Furthermore, nations and communities can suffer these crises too communities can suffer these crises too as they grow or respond to major changes. How a culture identifies itself and what it wants and holds dear can be part of a national identity crisis that may take a while to resolve and may be somewhat constantly in flux. This brings us to God and who we are in Him. Gen. 2: 15-18... The Lord God took the man and put him in the Garden of Eden to work it and take care of it. And the Lord God commanded the man, "You are free to eat from any tree in the garden; but you must not eat from the tree of knowledge of good and evil, for when you eat of it you will surely die." The Lord God said, "It is not good for the man to be alone. I will make a helper suitable for him. 1 Cor. 9:3 Now, I want you to realize that the Head of every man is Christ, and the Head of every woman is man, and the Head of Christ is God. Before the fall of Adam and Eve God set the stage for them in the Garden of Eden in perfect form and atmosphere. In the Garden there was perfect peace in the family setting; Adam was given authority over the earth and in Adams authority notice in scripture God created Adam as a man and not a child or a boy because a child or a boy would not fit in such an atmosphere of authority.

Only a man given authority by God would fit such a hierarchy position, now there are five things God gave Adam 1.) Eden....2.), Work....3.) Cultivation....4.), Protection....5.) Gods Command...but there is five things God did first with male and that is 1.) the first human God created was the male, 2.) The first thing God gave the male was his image, 3.) The first place God place the male was in the Garden of Eden, 4.) The first assignment God gave the male was work, 5.) The first instruction God gave the male was cultivate. Many of us coming up in looking at scripture believed that the first thing gave the male was dominion over the earth this is misinformation and has been the bases of the down fall of man's position and relationship on earth, is this attitude of authority first.

If you study the scripture more carefully you would discover that the first thing God decided was not how much power and authority man was going to have, the first thing God decided was man's identity and What is man's identity? "THE IMAGE OF GOD," It is in the image of God where all things in man starts, when a child is born the first thing parent identifies with is who the child looks like, as an teenager or an adult being a citizen of this nation of the United States it is a law that you obtain legal identification. Image is the essential key component of a man's life because image shapes character. As a citizen of the Kingdom of God being placed here on this earth you were given an identification to carry and be attached to you all the days of your life on earth and beyond "THE IMAGE OF GOD." This is to identify you as to what you are, why you are here, where you are going and How long you will be here. Adam was given the image of God, then instructions of what he was here for, Why he was here, Where he belong and how long he was to be in the garden "Eternally" (1000 years), until an identity crises struck the garden. Devil embodied in the image of the snake sought to bring about a false identity, starting with Adams wife Eve. The Bible says that the serpent was more crafty than any beast of the field which God had made and he said to the woman— "Indeed, has God said, you shall not eat from any tree of the garden?"

The woman of the garden said to the serpent, "From the fruit of the trees of the garden we may eat; but from the fruit of the tree which is in the middle of the garden, God has said, You shall not eat from it or touch it, or you will die." The serpent said to the woman, "You surely will not die! For God knows that in the day you eat from it your eyes will be opened and you will be like God, knowing good and evil." This is called "Identity Theft" when one seeks to rob you of what you posses, that you no longer posses it. Devil sought to take away Adams identity by manipulating his wife Eve to switch from knowing only the image of God, which "Good" to now knowing his image "Evil." Gen.3:1-5. This is "The Battle of the Culture" where many of us do not know who we are as we carry out our lives here on earth. Too many false identities labeled upon us than the righteous identity "Image of God", we are to raped up into these mediocre labels such as "African American," "European American," Asian American," "Latino American" all these different labels we honor and display upon ourselves beyond the "Image of God."

If you declare yourself to be of God, then you are a "CITIZEN OF THE KINGDOM OF GOD," first before you are anything else. The reason Africa is called mother and not father is because you came through Africa not from Africa. When you are born of a woman you come through the woman's womb not from the woman's womb. Life comes from the seed of your father not the egg of the woman, so Africa is not a "SEED" it is an "EGG." This is why it's called mother and not father, because Africa incubates life not produces life, God produces life, not a piece of land. I came through Africa, but from my Father in Heaven who is the "Author of Life." So any label you give yourself outside the "Image of God" is a false label and should not have any authority upon your life unless it is from God who gave you the life you have. For His purpose not your own purpose and plan, you don't know enough about this life to have your own purpose and plan, this is why God says to the people of Israel— "For My thoughts are not your thoughts, Nor are your ways My ways," declares the Lord. "For as the heavens are higher than the earth, so are my ways higher than your ways and my thoughts than your thoughts. Isa. 55:8; 9.

Once the fall of Adam and Eve too place, devil then presented a claim to Christ of owning the world as he said to Him— "I will give you all this domain and its glory; for it has been handed over to me, and I give it to whomever I wish. Therefore if you worship before me, it shall all be yours." Luke 4:6; 7. See, Devil committed identity theft upon Adam and Eve when the fall of them occurred because he was the cause of the "fall." This is the greatest level of theft that many people fast on a daily bases in this life is identity theft, having to deal with your name or your life being almost destroyed by such an act as this. The pain of the process to recover from such an act, pain in the initial thought process of the since of lost, which an overbearing mental pain that leads to a physical pain. This is how things play out in this "Battle of the Culture" when the Bible says— "We don't wrestle with flesh and blood but with spirits and principalities." Eph 6:12. The Devil seeks permission to attack our citizenship in the Kingdom of Heaven daily and his purpose is to keep us from knowing who we are in Christ. If we lose our identity in Christ, we lose ourselves; we lose ourselves on earth we lose our life from earth because at this point you are easily led to do anything as opposed to what the direction of God would be for the purpose he placed upon your life.

It is very important to know your intimate purpose in Christ, your purpose and plan is all a part of the "Image of God," why so much the "Image of God" because you are the seed of your Father and being your Fathers seed is vitally important too whom you look like. If Devil can get you to believe in who you aren't as he did Eve in the Garden then it becomes temporarily powerful for him to get you not to believe in who you are the "Image of God" first before dominion. This is why many miss what God is seeking to do in your life because of misinformation, false information that one can't get beyond. So many people are misinformed on how God work; many are seeking to identify themselves with some sort of image in life that they themselves can identify with. It is in the image of things that one seeks his or her identity, in a mediocre world and because of image the world loses sight about who it was created by and for therefore the world falls into an Abyss by way of the hand of God. Christ Jesus was sent for the restoration of the "Image of God" before freeing mankind from bondage, it was the image of God that appeared to be in more danger than man being in bondage. This is why the Bible says— "Meditate on God's word day and night, so that you may be careful to do according to all that is   written in it, what are we meditating on day and night, the overwhelming reason to such a high level of meditation is for purpose of God's Image. His Image as glorified as it is maintains all standards in your life know the level of intense character, integrity, discipline, obedience and righteousness such that this 'Image of God" carries it has no room for many crisis. Crisis come only by way of the opposite of what Gods image stands for and the opposite of God's Image is simple wickedness or foolishness. But often times God uses crisis to bring us to a point of obedience that "His Image" can shape our lives that looking upon us will see God in our thinking, our attitude, our speech, our behavior and our action. This is why crisis is important to identify, to know which way God is going with the use of the crisis in our lives, to know what the moment of the crisis is for, why the crisis exist and how to apply the wisdom of solution to the crisis that it "works for the good of those who love the Lord." A crisis is not something we have many answers too, we often fall short in dealing with crisis effectively enough that this crisis does not return the same way twice. Crisis must be met with head on with only God given wisdom, that the spirits and principalities that enforces a crisis can be met with very Holy Spirit that will give you the power of resistant's and the ability to overcome the obstacles that accompany it.

You must not allow any room for crisis to over shadow the "Image of God" in you at no point for the sake of growth, progress, character etc. You must live your life in these last days as if Christ is returning tonight, seeking or pursuing God knowing He holds your life in the balance of His hands, under constant protection from the wolves, jackals and snakes. For any attack that comes to our lives must first get permission, can you imagine that, your enemy must get permission to put his hands upon you. What an awesome God we serve, "I MEAN AWSOME." You must know and understand meaning of a demonic spirit having to get permission to touch your life, do you understand how powerful that is, and the process a "Demonic Force" has to go through to get to you. What crisis could you possibly experience without the hand of God not being a part of things to protect your life. Identity Crisis is not a means of destruction; it's a means of opportunity, an opportune time in God obedience, discipline, character and integrity which should bring about a perfect union with God. But because of many not feeding the mind the proper level of God's word that your thinking is dealt with and changed so much so that discipline is the ruling aspect of your thought process. The main reason that we miss out on much of Gods directions in our lives is that we lack the kind of discipline in our thinking process, which would bring our decisions to a complete "YEA" and "NEA," anything beyond that is of the Devil the Bible says. Crisis should bring you growth from the level it began to the level it forces you to, why by force simply because of many of our stiff neck ways we allow to take root or stronghold in our thinking causing us to disobey Gods directions. The Bibles says— "Many are the plans in a man's heart but God directs his steps," Prov. 16:9. Crisis come by way of misinformation or no directions, we to many times find ourselves listening to our outer man instead of the inner man as the great "Marvin Gaye" would sing and that's where we fall in much trouble during the course of our lives. God continues to hammer away at our stubbornness to follow his instructions and many refuse to hear His voice or just not intimate enough with God to even hear His voice. Many bring about great damage control in their lives that in some cases it is beyond repair. We are in a time frame where it must be Gods way or you will be removed, we will begin to see that revolving door of the days when God remove you from for sin and those days are returning especially now that grace is on the scene through Christ.

God no longer has to keep folk on earth to assure ones inheritage through a series of faith walks and prophetic deeds, Christ has covered all our sins of yesterday, today and tomorrow we no longer are in need of the New Moon Festival and Sin Offerings, we have been sealed with the Holy Spirit that guarantee our salvation upon our confession of Rom. 10:9. So to remove those who are in great disobedience God will do and is doing to keep many from loosing portions of their inheritage. For it is your inheritage that is the only thing from Heaven that you will lose parts of and the Bibles says that God loves us so, that he protects us from taking great lost of our inheritage. The most powerful and richest place on earth is the cemetery simply because so many persons have left this earth without fulfilling the purpose God gave to many to serve here on earth. So many ideas, inventions, cure for diseases, answers to things in this life that would change the course of time forever. All in the cemetery not even an ounce of time to exercise such power and authority that was placed in these persons in the unique way they were created to exercise. So we lose those possibilities to bring about other persons with God given capabilities to exercise their uniqueness of gifting being shown to the world that the purpose of God can prevail. Prevail in a supernatural way that we can make great strive in this life just as God is calling us to have, not slothful or slumbered and full of poverty but making the difference in the lives of your family, friends and neighbors as we were chosen to do so. A nation of doers not a nation of Ney-Sayers but to conform in God that the world can spot who you are not by a cross on your neck or a bumper sticker, but in your speech, your walk, letting that spirit of God within us so connect to the Holy Spirit, that the directions and instruction given to us from God, by way of Christ in which direct the Holy Spirit to bring life into all things. We are to carry out the same as to what the Holy Spirit has been given because he is in us to do so, so that which is in you must flow out of you in righteousness that the world is affected by it so greatly that God is honored and Glorified in the Majestic manner that He demands. We are the Kings Royal Priesthood and we were chosen to operate in the "Image of God" and have dominion over this "Earth," NOT TO CREATE AN IDENTITY CRISIS"

In this life we must not focus on our circumstances. That is a biblical principle that "you do not look to the bigness of your circumstances but look to the bigness of God, for if you look to the bigness of your circumstances then the Devil will use that moment against you and accuse you before God of lack of faith and belief in God to by o you to grace protect and bring you relief of that which stands in your way," We are to look past our circumstances in fact we are not too recognize our circumstances. We are to commit our lives so great too the purpose and plan that God has place upon you and live the meaning of that which God gave to carry out here on earth. Any and everyone has a purpose here and it isn't "Crisis," that is what is used to put us in obedience or discipline in God that character and integrity rules. You must live by meaning, What does your life mean to you? Is it a game or joke? Is it real? What is your name? Call your name and see what you are known by. These things are meaning, in my life I know I am to make a difference in the lives of others, that's something stuck with me all my life as I went through my daily routines of just getting up to go to a meaningless job. Faced with every day crisis I was lost in identity in my youth, but always had the spirit to help someone, something that I watch my "Mama" and my "Grandma" do. It was not something that I recognize as my purpose it was just something that was in me to do as the days of my life went forth as a youth. The day came when becoming a part of different communities and new persons arose in my life that I began to discover the meaning behind wanting to help folk. It began to unravel not in your typical world like fashion where you are in the streets and someone just think they know you well enough to tell you about your life "No." It came by way of the life I lived in God, see, I realize by way of the intimacy I have with God automatically gives the Holy Spirit the access it need to bring us wisdom even when we don't ask for it. You think you pick up on some high level of "ESP" as the world would say that gave you insight to the life we live, but the Bible says God through Christ Jesus is the author and giver of life period. Who else then can inform you of life but the author and giver of it? As I began to investigate my life more it came to my attention that I have a real purpose here on earth and how did I find it, by the greatest question ever ask of me "What is your Passion in Life"? I stop a moment and had to put in some heavy meditation about that and of course the devil took root to that thought and began to squander my mind everywhere.

I went after that question upon my own notion that I knew what I was searching for and found myself bringing on a headache, until I denied me and ask the Lord for the wisdom in this thing and as I began to remove me in thought. My though patterns began to open up to me and who I am and the thing I enjoy to do. That is help people, to make a difference in lives of people, I recognize the energy and strength I put into such a meaningful cause. Once I   realize what this meant in my life, this was it, this is my passion, and this is my "Purpose." I began to feed this thing and bring it more to life as it must be, I studied Gods word on this and learn a deeper meaning on how it works from Gods point of view since He put it in me then the one to ask is the one who gave it "God," my life began to take a turn from "Identity Crisis" to "True Identity," the "Image of God." But once knowing this you would think life got better no, greater struggle, greater difficulty and greater attack. Why? Because we were in Devil's camp having a ball enjoying the world's lifestyle, chasing the wind of sex, lies and videotapes, festering in Devils mess, believing this was our way of life to live. When we were actually as to what the word of God says— whoever wishes to be a friend of the world makes himself an enemy of God. This is where we are when we are not with God, we are against God and that's the reason for attack, struggle and Identity Crisis, we lose sight of God and become someone we were not purpose to be and so the hand of God come against you is enemy. When you step out of Devils kingdom then you become an enemy of Devil, in other words there is no neutral zone between Gods Kingdom and Devils kingdom. You are in one or the other and either way you face difficulty, but the difference in Gods difficulty and Devils difficulty is with God difficulty come grace, peace and official rest as long as you remain in Him. This means that most income groups have experienced consistent increases in income. In the USA the most affluent part of the population has experienced the strongest income growth and the median income in the USA has consequently increased less than in Denmark. The higher degree of income inequality in the USA may help explain the registered fall in life satisfaction. It was the interest and business of the medieval thirteen colonies to study and conquer human nature, and the labor of a slave in particular, with a broad view to a powerful result. Most of these colonies attained astonishing economic proficiency in this direction.

They had to deal not with the nature of earth and its resources, but with men and, by every regard, they had their own economic safety net and prosperity they needed to know the path to which was a must to take, conscious of the injustice and wrong they were every hour perpetuating and knowing what they themselves must do. Fearing becoming the victims of such wrongs, they were constantly looking for the day of the dreaded retribution. They watched therefore with skilled and practiced eyes, and learned to read with great accuracy, the state of mind and heart of the slave, through his stern face. Unusual human strength and indifference indeed, any act of common sense was ground for suspicion and inquiry. Frederick Douglas LET'S MAKE A SLAVE is a study of the scientific process of man-breaking and slave-making. It describes the rationale and results of the Anglo Saxons' ideas and methods of insuring the master/slave relationship. **LET'S MAKE A SLAVE** "The Original and Development of a Social Being. Now today being called **'The Making Of A Prosperous Slave Nation."** What did they need? First of all, They needed a black male preacher, a black man, a pregnant black woman and her baby boy. Second, they had to use the same basic principle that they used in breaking a horse, a mule or a bull combined with some more sustaining factors. But they revised the horse title to simply the title of nigger and the black man do to uneducated and educational advancement in breaking them both like a horse from one form of life to another; that is, they reduce them from their natural state in nature, family unification, land & property ownership as well as self worth economics. Whereas the hand of GOD provides the indigenous black man & woman with the earth's natural resources and the skills & abilities to take care of their family, friends and neighbors, they break the divine order of independence from them and thereby create a western colonial world dependency status, so that they may be able to sift from this prosperous slave useful productivity for greater business and pleasure. For fear that the future colonial generations may not understand the principles of breaking this indigenous black man, woman together to be reduced to a nigger, like a horse they understood that short range planning economics results in periodic economic chaos; so that to avoid turmoil in the economy, it required them to have established economic depth in long range comprehensive planning, articulating both skills and sharp perceptions.

They laid down the foundation principles for long range comprehensive economic planning. Both educated black men and/or niggers are no good to the western colonial economy in the wilds of life or natural state. Both must be **BROKEN, REDUCED AND PIT** together for orderly production. For orderly future, special and particular attention had to be paid to the **BLACK FEMALE** and the **YOUNGEST MAN CHILD**. Both had to be **CROSSBRED** to produce a variety and division of labor. Both had to be taught to respond to a peculiar new **LANGUAGE**. Psychological and physical instruction of **CONTAINMENT** had to be created for both. They had to create six cardinal principles as truth to be self-evident, based upon following the discourse concerning the economics of breaking , reducing, tying the black man and the nigger together like animals, all inclusive of the six principles laid down above. Neither principle alone will suffice for good economics. All principles must be employed for orderly good in the making of a prosperous slave nation. Accordingly, both a wild nigger(negus African King) or a natural indigenous black man(Dynasty or Empire) is dangerous even if captured, for they will have the tendency to seek their divine freedom and, in doing so, might kill the colonial Anglo-Saxon man or woman in their sleep. So they could not rest. The black man and woman sleep while the Anglo-Saxon men & women are awake, and studying the world population. The black man and woman is said to be dangerous near the Anglo-Saxons family house and it requires too much labor to watch them away from the house. Above all, one cannot get them to work in this natural state. Henceforth, both the black man and the nigger must be broken, and reduced that is breaking the nigger and reducing the black man to keep both of them from one form of mental life to another. **KEEP THE BODY, DESTROY THE MIND!** In other words, break the will to resist. In the same breaking process you would a horse, only slightly varying in degrees. But, as it was said before, there is an art in long range economic planning. **YOU MUST KEEP YOUR EYE AND THOUGHTS ON THE BLACK FEMALE and the MAN CHILD** of the black man and nigger. A brief discourse in offspring development will shed light on the key element of things. Pay little attention to the generation of original breaking, but **CONCENTRATE ON FUTURE GENERATION**.

Therefore, if you break the **BLACK FEMALE** mother away from the black male economic dependency, giving her economic independency, she will **BREAK** the offspring the same manner in its early years of development; and when the offspring is old enough to work, they will psychologically be deliver it up to being economically dependent upon the western colonial practices. For her normal female protective tendencies will have been lost in the colonial economic independency process. For example, take the case of the wild stud horse, a female horse and an already infant horse and compare the breaking process with two captured nigger males in their natural state, a pregnant nigger woman with her infant offspring. Take the stud horse, break him for limited containment. Completely break the female horse until she becomes very gentle, whereas you or anybody can ride her in her comfort. Breed the mare and the stud until you have the desired offspring. Then, you can turn the stud to freedom until you need him again. Train the female horse whereby she will eat out of your hand, and she will in turn train the infant horse to eat out of your hand, also. When it comes to breaking the indigenous black man, use the same process, but vary the degree and step up the pressure, so as to do a complete reduction of the mind. Take the meanest and most uncivilized nigger, strip him of his dignity as a man in front of the indigenous black man and the black woman, and the young, kill his pride, destroy his manhood and treat him like a horse placed under strict instructions that brings about anger and harshly discipline him in front of the masses of the people. This step will be like a bullwhip beating the nigger males to the point of mental death, in front of the female and the youth. Designed not to kill him, but **PUT THE FEAR OF GOD IN HIM**, for he can be useful for future prosperous labor. Take the black female and run a series of tests on her to see if she will submit to colonial rule willingly. Test her in every way, because she is the most important factor for good economics. If she shows any sign of resistance in submitting completely to colonial will, do not hesitate to use the threat of economic demise on her to extract that last bit of nigger woman out of her. Take care not to damage her emotionally, for in doing so, you spoil good economic labor. When in complete submission, she will train her offspring's in the early years to submit to all labor of any condition when they become of age. Understanding is the best thing. Therefore, They shall go deeper into this area of the subject matter concerning what has been produced here in this breaking process of the black female to a good nigger woman.

You have reversed the relationship; in her natural civilized state, she would have a strong dependency on the civilized black man, and she would have a unlimited protective tendency toward her dependent male offspring and would raise male offspring's to be independent like his parenting black male. Nature had provided for this type of balance but in reversing nature by reducing a indigenous black man to an uncivilized nigger and mentally bullwhipping a uncivilized nigger to the point of mental death, all in her presence. By her being left alone, unprotected, with the **INDIGENOUS BLACK MALE IMAGE DESTROYED**, the ordeal caused her to move from her psychologically dependent state to a frozen, independent state. In this frozen, psychological state of independence, she will raise her **MALE** and female offspring in reversed roles. For **FEAR** of the young male's life, she will psychologically train him to be **MENTALLY WEAK** and **DEPENDENT**, but **PHYSICALLY STRONG**. Because she has become psychologically independent, she will train her **FEMALE** offspring's to be psychologically independent. What have you got? You've got the nigger **WOMAN OUT FRONT AND THE** nigger **MAN BEHIND AND SCARED**. This is a perfect ingredient of **THE MAKING OF A PROSPEROUS SLAVE NATION** and lasting economics. Before the breaking process, it had to be an alertly on guard at all times moment. Now, one can sleep soundly, for out of frozen fear the nigger woman stands guard for the advancement of colonial economics. The man child cannot get past his early slave molding & fashioning process. He is a good tool, now ready to be tied to the labor force at a tender age. By the time a nigger boy reaches the age of sixteen, he is soundly broken in and ready for a long life of sound and efficient slave labor and the reproduction of a unit of good labor force jobs. Continually through the breaking of uncivilized savage niggers, by throwing the nigger female savage into a frozen psychological state of independence, by killing the protective black male image, and by creating a submissive dependent mind of the nigger male slave, the colonial Anglo-Saxon society have created an orbiting cycle that turns on its own axis forever, unless a phenomenon occurs and re-shifts the position of the black male and female slaves.

Colonial experts have warned the possibility of this phenomenon occurring, for they say that the mind of the black man has a strong drive to correct and re-correct itself over a period of time if it can touch some substantial original historical base; and it was advised that the best way to deal with the phenomenon is to shave off the brute's mental history and create a multiplicity of phenomena of illusions, so that each illusion will twirl in its own orbit, something similar to floating balls in a vacuum. This creation of multiplicity of phenomena of illusions entails the principle of crossbreeding the wild nigger, the purpose of which is to create a diversified division of labor; thereby creating different levels
of labor and different values of illusion at each connecting level of labor. The results of which is the severance of the points of original beginnings for each sphere illusion. Since its felt that the subject matter may get more complicated as it proceed in laying down colonial ruled economic plan concerning the purpose, reason and effect of crossbreeding indigenous minded black men & women with uncivilized niggers, we shall lay down the following definition terms for future generations. Orbiting cycle means a thing turning in a given path. Axis means upon which or around which a body turns. Phenomenon means something beyond ordinary conception and inspires awe and wonder. Multiplicity means a great number. Means a globe. Crossbreeding a horse means taking a horse(indigenous black man or woman) and breeding it with an ass(wild nigger man or woman) and you get a dumb, backward, ass long-headed mule that is not reproductive nor productive by itself. Crossbreeding niggers mean taking so many drops of good white blood and putting them into as many nigger women as possible, varying the drops by the various tone that you want, and then letting them breed with each other until another circle of color appears as you desire. What this means is this: Put the niggers and the horse in a breeding pot, mix some asses and some good white blood and what do you get? You got a multiplicity of colors of ass backward, unusual niggers, running, tied to backward ass long-headed mules, the one productive of itself, the other sterile. (The one constant, the other dying, we keep the nigger constant for we may replace the mules(dumb nigger) for another tool both mule(dumb nigger) and nigger tied to each other, neither knowing where the other came from and neither productive for itself, nor without each other. In other words create the world's wealthiest nation of slave laborers for a high colonial economic gain.

Crossbreeding completed, for further severance from their original beginning, **THERE MUST BE A COMPLETE ANNIHILATION OF INDEPENDENT CORPORATE ECONOMIC OPORTUNITY** of both the new nigger and the new mule(dumb nigger), and institute a new language that involves the new life of colonial dependent economics of both. You know language is a peculiar institution. It leads to the heart of a people. The more a foreigner knows about the language of another country the more he is able to move through all levels of that society. Therefore, if the foreigner is an enemy of the country, to the extent that he knows the body of the language, to that extent is the country vulnerable to attack or invasion of a foreign culture. For example, if you take a slave, if you teach him all about your language, he will know all your secrets, and he is then no more a slave, for you can't fool him any longer, and **BEING A FOOL IS ONE OF THE BASIC INGREDIENTS OF ANY INCIDENTS TO THE MAINTENANCE OF THE SLAVERY SYSTEM**. If you told a slave that he must perform in getting out "our crops" and he knows the language well, he would know that "our crops" didn't mean "our crops" and the slavery system would break down, for he would relate on the basis of what "our crops" really meant. So you have to be careful in setting up the new language; for the slaves would soon be in your house, talking to you as "man to man" and that is death to the colonial rule economic system. In addition, the definitions of words or terms are only a minute part of the process. Values are created and transported by communication through the body of the language. A total society has many interconnected value systems. All the values in the society have bridges of language to connect them for orderly working in the society. But for these language bridges, these many value systems would sharply clash and cause internal strife or civil war, the degree of the conflict being determined by the magnitude of the issues or relative opposing strength in whatever form. If you put a slave in a hog pen and train him to live there and incorporate in him to value it as a way of life completely, the biggest problem you would have out of him is that he would worry you about provisions to keep the hog pen clean, or the same hog pen and make a slip and incorporate something in his language whereby he comes to value a house more than he does his hog pen, you got a problem and he will soon be in your house of rule. To which is the black man's origin BUILDING YOUR OWN SAND BOX al position is to have dominion over the earth.

CHAPTER V

The World's Wealthiest Nation

Black America, Impact of the
Great Depression

The Great Depression brought mass suffering to all regions of the country. National income dropped by 50 percent and <u>unemployment</u> rose to an estimated 25 percent of the total <u>labor force</u>. At the same time, twenty million Americans turned to public and private relief agencies for assistance. As the "Last Hired and the First Fired," <u>Black Americans</u> entered the Depression long before the stock market crash in 1929, and they stayed there longer than other Americans. By 1933, African Americans found it all but impossible to find jobs of any kind in <u>agriculture</u> or industry. As cotton prices dropped from eighteen cents per pound on the eve of the Depression to less than six cents per pound in 1933, some 12,000 black sharecroppers lost their precarious footing in southern agriculture and moved increasingly toward southern, northern, and western cities. Mechanical devices had already slowly reduced the number of workers required for plowing, hoeing, and weeding, but now planters also experimented with mechanical cotton pickers, which displace more black farm workers. Despite declining opportunities in cities, the proportion of blacks living in urban areas rose from 44 percent in 1930 to nearly 50 percent by the onset of World War II. As the number of rural blacks seeking jobs in cities escalated, urban black workers experienced increasing difficulties. Black urban unemployment reached well over 50 percent, more than twice the rate of whites. In southern cities, white workers rallied around such slogans as, "No Jobs for Niggers Until Every White Man Has a Job" and "Niggers, back to the cotton fields—city jobs are for white folks." The most violent episodes took place on southern railroads, as unionized white workers and the railroad brotherhoods intimidated, attacked, and murdered black firemen in order to take their jobs Nearly a dozen black firemen lost their jobs in various parts of the South. As one contemporary observer succinctly stated, "The shotgun, the whip, the noose, and Ku Klux Klan practices were being resumed in the certainty that dead men not only tell no tales, but create vacancies." For their part, in the North and South, black women were forced into the notorious Depression era "slave market," where even working-class white women employed black women at starvation wages, as little as $5 per week for full- time laborers in northern cities.

In their studies of the market in Bronx, New York, two black women compared the practice to the treatment of slaves in Harriet Beecher Stowe's novel Uncle Tom's Cabin. Despite mass suffering, the Republican administration of Herbert Hoover did little to aid the poor and destitute. Instead, the federal government established the Reconstruction Finance Corporation, which relieved the credit problems of large banking, insurance, and industrial firms. Although Hoover believed that such policies would create new jobs, stimulate production, and increase consumer spending, benefits did not "trickle down" to the rest of the economy and end the Depression. Still, Black Americans rallied to the slogan "Who but Hoover" in the presidential contest of 1932. In the eyes of blacks, the Republican Party remained the party of emancipation, partly because Democratic candidate Franklin Delano Roosevelt had embraced the segregationist policies of the Democratic Party. Following his inauguration, Roosevelt's attitude toward Black Americans changed little. He not only opposed vital civil rights legislation like the anti-lynching bill, designed to make lynching a federal offense, but showed little interest in challenging even the most blatant manifestations of racial injustice in the proliferation of New Deal agencies. The National Recovery Administration (NRA), Agricultural Adjustment Administration (AAA), the Works Progress Administration (WPA), the Tennessee Valley Authority (TVA), the Civilian Conservation Corps (CCC), and the Federal Emergency Relief Administration (FERA), to name only a few, all failed to protect blacks against discriminatory employers, agency officials, and local whites. When the AAA had paid farmers systematically to withdraw the cotton lands from production, county officials barred Black Americans from representation and deprived them of government checks. For their part, by exempting domestic service and unskilled labor from minimum wage and participatory provisions, the NRA and the social security programs eliminated nearly 60 percent of African Americans from benefits. When the jobs of African Americans were brought under the provisions of the NRA in southern textile firms, employers reclassified such jobs and removed them from coverage of the higher wage code. As they encountered various forms of discrimination in New Deal Agencies, many African Americans concluded that the so-called New Deal was indeed a "raw deal." Only during the mid-1930s would Black Americas gain broader access to the New Deal social programs.

By 1939, income from New Deal work and relief programs nearly matched African-American income from private employment. Black Americas occupied about one-third of all federal low-income housing projects, and gained a growing share of CCC jobs, Federal Farm Security loans, and benefits from WPA educational and cultural programs. Black Americas now frequently hailed the New Deal as "a godsend." Some blacks even quipped that God "will lead me" and relief "will feed me." The emergence of a "new deal" for blacks was closely intertwined with the growth of the Communist Party, the resurgence of organized labor, and the increasing political efforts of blacks on their own behalf. When the Communist Party helped save nine black youths, the Scottsboro Boys, from execution and secured the release of their own black comrade Angelo Herndon from a Georgia chain gang, the Black-Americas community took notice. When the party helped to initiate hunger marches, unemployed councils, farm labor unions, rent strikes, and mass demonstrations to prevent the eviction of black families from their homes, its work had gained greater recognition within the Black Americas community. As one black newspaper editor, of the Amsterdam News, reported, "The fight that they are putting up . . . strike forcefully at the fundamental wrongs suffered by the Negro today." The rise of the Congress of Industrial Organizations (CIO) in 1935 facilitated the emergence of a real New Deal for African Americans. Unlike the old American Federation of Labor (AFL), the CIO made a firm commitment to organize both black and white workers. The organization soon launched the Packinghouse Workers Organizing Committee (PWOC), the United Automobile Workers (UAW), and the Steel Workers Organizing Committee (SWOC). The new unions appealed to civil rights organizations like the National Association for the Advancement of Colored People (NAACP) and the Urban League, recruited black organizers, and advocated an end to unequal pay scales for black and white workers. Although most AFL unions continued to exclude black workers, the national leadership gradually supported a more equitable stance toward black workers. The union finally approved an international charter for the Brotherhood of Sleeping Car Porters (BSCP) in 1935 and endorsed efforts to free the Scottsboro Boys and Angelo Herndon. Following the lead of anthropologist Franz Boas and his associates, social scientists encouraged the lowering of racial barriers in Americas society.

As early as the 1920s, they had gradually turned away from earlier biological definitions of race, which defined African Americans as innately inferior. The new social scientists challenged the biological determinists to "prove" that Black Americas occupied a lower socioeconomic and political status in American society because of their hereditary inferiority. Legal change lagged significantly behind the new intellectual perspectives on race; yet, even here, African Americans witnessed the slow transition to a new deal. As early as 1935, the Maryland Court of Appeals ordered the University of Maryland to admit blacks to the state's law school or set up a new separate and equal facility for blacks. Rather than face the expense of establishing a new all-black law school, university officials lowered racial barriers and admitted black students to the all-white institution. Despite the rise of interracial alliances and the emergence of anti-racist movements among whites, Black Americas developed their own strategies for social change and helped to create their own "new deal." Black Americas cared for each other's children, offered emotional support, and creatively manipulated their family's resources. As one Georgia relief official noted, "These people are catching and selling fish, reselling vegetables, sewing in exchange for old clothes, letting out sleeping space, and doing odd jobs . . . Stoves are used in common, wash boilers go their rounds, and garden crops are exchanged and shared." Urban blacks also maintained vegetable gardens, staged rent parties, played the numbers game, and expanded their church-based social welfare activities. While rent parties provided "down home" food, drink, music, and a place to dance for a small admission fee, the "policy" or numbers game employed large numbers of Black Americas as runners and as bookkeepers. According to some observers, for example, Chicago's south side employed seven thousand people in the numbers business and cushioned them from unemployment even as it provided hope for thousands of blacks seeking to make a "hit." For their part, some "numbers kings" provided donations to black churches and charitable organizations, but religious organizations launched their own social welfare activities. In addition to the work of established denominations, new religious movements also expanded their efforts to feed the poor. Started during the 1920s, for example, Father Divine's Peace Mission moved its headquarters from Sayville on Long Island to Harlem in 1932 and gained credit for feeding the masses and offering relief from widespread destitution.

At about the same time, Bishop Charles Emmanuel Grace, known as "Daddy Grace," founded the United House of Prayer of All People, opened offices in twenty cities, and offered thousands of people respite from suffering. As African Americans used their community based social networks and institutions to address their needs, they also turned toward the labor movement. Under the growing influence of the new CIO unions, African Americans expanded their place in the house of labor. Perhaps more than any other single figure, however, A. Philip Randolph epitomized the persistent struggle of black workers to organize in their own interests. Born in Crescent City, Florida, in 1889, Randolph had migrated to New York City in 1911 and spearheaded the formation of the Brotherhood of Sleeping Car Porters and Maids in 1925. When New Deal federal legislation (the Railway Labor Act of 1934) legitimized the rights of workers to organize, Randolph and the BSCP intensified its organizing drive among black porters. By 1933, the union represented some 35,000 porters. Two years later, the union defeated a company union and won the right to represent porters at the bargaining table with management, which signed its first contract with the union in 1937. The BSCP victory not only helped to make African Americans more union conscious, but increased their impact on national labor policy. The NAACP, Urban League, and other civil rights organizations also increased their focus on the economic plight of African Americans. In 1933, these organizations formed the Joint Committee on National Recovery (JCNR) and helped to publicize the racial inequities in New Deal programs. Black Americas also launched the "Don't Buy Where You Can't Work" campaign in New York, Chicago, Washington, D. C., and other cities. They boycotted white merchants who served the Black Americas community but refused to employ blacks except in domestic and common laborer positions. When Harlem store owners refused to negotiate, New York blacks formed the Citizens League for Fair Play and set up pickets around Blumstein's Department Store. In 1938, their actions produced concrete results when the New York Uptown Chamber of Commerce and the Greater New York Coordinating Committee for Employment agreed to give Black Americas one-third of all new retail executive, clerical, and sales jobs. African Americans usually expressed their grievances through organized and peaceful action, but sometimes they despaired and turned to violence. Racial violence erupted in Harlem in 1935 when a rumor spread that a black youth had been brutally attacked and killed by police.

Although the rumor proved false, African-American crowds soon gathered and smashed buildings and looted stores in a night of violence that left one person dead, over fifty injured, and thousands of dollars in property damage. Some blacks believed that radicalism offered the most appropriate response to the deepening crisis of African Americans. Some African Americans joined the Socialist Southern Tenant Farmers Union (STFU) and the Communist Alabama Sharecroppers Union. Nate Shaw (Ned Cobb), whose life became the subject of an oral biography, recalled that he had joined the sharecroppers union to fight the system that oppressed him. Shaw later recalled that he had to act because he had labored "under many rulins, just like the other Negro, that I knowed was injurious to man and displeasin to God and still I had to fall back." In Birmingham, the Communist Party's League of Struggle for Negro Rights (LSNR) and its energetic fight on behalf of the Scottsboro Boys also attracted unemployed workers, such as Al Murphy and Hosea Hudson. As Hudson put it, "I always did resent injustice and the way they used to treat Negroes....My grandmother used to talk about these things. She was very militant herself, you know."

BLACKS AND THE NEW DEAL
COALITION

Although some blacks joined radical social movements and parties, most worked hard to broaden their participation in the New Deal coalition. As Republicans continued to take black votes for granted, blacks increasingly turned toward the northern wing of the Democratic Party. As early as 1932, the editor of the black weekly Pittsburgh Courier had urged Black Americas to change their political affiliation: "My friends, go turn Lincoln's picture to the wall . . . that debt has been paid in full." By the mid-1930s, nearly forty-five blacks had received appointments to New Deal agencies. Referred to as the Black Cabinet, these black advisors included Robert L. Vann, editor of the Pittsburgh Courier, Robert C. Weaver, an economist, and Mary McCleod Bethune, founder of Bethune-Cookman College in Florida. In 1936, African Americans formed the National Negro Congress (NNC), which aimed to unite all existing political, fraternal, and religious organizations and push for policies designed to bring about the full socioeconomic recovery of the black community.

Spearheaded by Ralph Bunche, a professor of political science at Howard University in Washington, D.C, and John Davis, executive secretary of the Joint Committee on National Recovery, the founding meeting of the NNC brought together some six hundred organizations and selected A. Philip Randolph as its first president. The NNC symbolized as well as promoted the growing political mobilization of the African-American community. In the presidential election of 1936, African Americans voted for the Democratic Party in record numbers; Roosevelt received 76 percent of northern black votes. After the election of 1936, African Americans intensified demands on Roosevelt's New Deal administration. They placed justice before the law high on their list of priorities. As early as 1933, the NAACP organized a Writers League Against Lynching and intensified its national movement for a federal anti-lynching law. The Cosigns-Wagner anti-lynching bill gained little support from Roosevelt and failed when southern senators filibustered the measure in 1934, 1935, 1937, 1938, and 1940. Despite failure to pass a federal anti-lynching law, partly because of the campaign, the number of recorded lynching's dropped from eighteen in 1935 to two in 1939. During the 1930s, black attorneys like Charles Hamilton Houston and William Hastie assaulted the legal supports of Jim Crow, while black historians, social scientists, and writers challenged its intellectual underpinnings. Under the leadership of historian Carter G. Woodson, the Association for the Study of Negro Life and History (founded in 1915) continued to promote the study of African-American history, emphasizing the role of blacks in the development of the nation. Black Americas intellectuals (E. Franklin Frazier, W. E. B. Du Bois, Charles S. Johnson, Langston Hughes, and Richard Wright) reinforced the work of Carter G. Woodson. As suggested by the role of black intellectuals and attorneys on the one hand and the rent parties of poor and working-class blacks on the other, Black Americas responses to poverty were by no means uniform. They varied across class, gender, and generational lines. Women manipulated household resources, while black men predominated in the organized labor and civil rights movements. Moreover, elite men dominated the leadership positions of civil rights and social service organizations like the NAACP and the Urban League. Yet, Black Americas during the period were united through a common history, color, and culture.

The emergence of Joe Louis as a folk hero symbolized African Americans' sense of common plight, kinship, and future. The exploits of Louis helped to unify Black Americas and gave them hope that they could demolish the segregationist system. When Joe Louis lost, Black Americas lamented, as in his first fight with the German Max Schmeling, who symbolized Adolf Hitler's doctrine of Aryan supremacy. When Louis knocked out Max Schmeling in the first round of their rematch, black people celebrated. The singer Lena Horne later recalled that Joe Louis "was the one invincible Negro, the one who stood up to the white man and beat him down with his fists. He in a sense carried so many of our hopes, maybe even dreams of vengeance." Despite the transition from a raw deal to a new deal between 1935 and 1939, the persistence of racial discrimination within and outside governmental agencies limited the achievements of the Roosevelt administration. As whites returned to full- time employment during the late 1930s, African Americans remained dependent on public service and relief programs. While the CIO aided blacks who were fortunate enough to maintain or regain their jobs during the Depression years, it did little to enhance the equitable reemployment of black and white workers as the country slowly pulled itself out of the Depression. The Communist Party helped to change attitudes toward racial unity, but the benefits of such changes were largely symbolic as racial injustice continued to undermine the material position of Black Americas. As the nation increasingly mobilized for War after 1939, African Americans resolved that World War II would be fought on two fronts. They wanted a "Double-V," victory at home and victory abroad. Recessions hurt. And they hurt the poor and socially marginalized populations the most. As we face the prospect of the second recession of the decade and consider the merits of various stimulus packages, it is useful to examine what a recession would mean for black America. The late 1990s produced a full employment economy and significant absolute and relative economic gains for blacks. This Issue Brief contrasts the benefits of a national full-employment economy with the harm caused by the 2001 recession and the weak job growth that followed. In the best of times, many African American communities are forced to tolerate levels of unemployment unseen in most white communities.

The 2001 recession pushed the white annual unemployment rate up from a low of 3.5% in 2000 to a high of 5.2% in 2003. During the same period, the black unemployment rate shot up from 7.6% to 10.8%. National recessions take African Americans from a bad situation to a worse one. In 2007, the black unemployment rate was 8.3%. A figure that black community still face the above the pre-recession low and more than twice the white unemployment rate. Goldman Sachs made an estimates that a new recession would increase the national unemployment rate to 6.4% by 2009. For Black Americas; the unemployment rate was expected to rise to 11.0%. The low unemployment rates of the 1990s led to positive gains in the black/white income ratio. In 1995, the median black family earned 60.9% of what the median white family did. By 2000, the ratio had climbed to a record high of 63.5%. The effect of the 2001 recession and the weak economic recovery was to undo all of those gains and then take away some more. By 2005, the median black household earned only 60.2% of the median white household, 0.7 points lower than it was in 1995. But median family income did not tell the entire story. The 2001 recession and weak recovery hurt the poorest black family the most. In 1995, the poorest fifth of black families only earned on average 43.0% of what the poorest fifth of white families earned. Again, the economic growth of the late 1990s was a significant boon. The black/white average income ratio for the poorest fifth increased to 49.9% in 2000. As reported by 2005, it had fallen back to 43.4%. Among blacks, the poorest black families lost the largest share of their income gains from the late 1990s. Another recession would reduce the median family income for all Americans by about 4%. However, for the black community, the decline was about 6%, leaving the average black families $2,400 poorer. This loss of income only hurt the poorest fifth of the black families the most. Associated with a strong economy of the 1990s, there were significant declines in the black violent crime rate and the black teen pregnancy rate. Between 1993 and 2001, black violent crime rate had declined by 60%. Between 1990 and 2004, the black teen pregnancy rate had declined by 46%. These so call improving trends had ended, and it was likely that the worsening economic conditions of the black families since 2001 had played at least a partial role.

At the community level, criminologists found a correlation between violent crime rates and social economic disadvantage. At the national level, too, the black violent crime rate had been strongly correlated with black poverty rates as well. Therefore, it was not surprising that the historic crime rates decline in the 1990s and ended with a reversal of economic fortunes that the black community experienced at the beginning of the 21st century. Based on a study of five countries including the United States, the Alan Guttmacher Institute reports "across all of the focus countries, young people growing up in disadvantaged economic, family and social circumstances were more likely than their better-off peers to engage in risky behavior and have a child during adolescence." Based on that social economic disadvantage had made an increased for the black family since 2000, it is not entirely surprising that black teen pregnancy rates had started to rise once again. Another recession was likely to continue these negative trends. The black male violent crime rate and the black teenage pregnancy rate both had rose over the years time. Once again, the negative effects of these trends had hurt the poorest of black families the most in time. Even when the national unemployment picture was good, the black community unemployment rate was more than twice that of the white unemployment rate. This meant that in what looked to be good economic times nationally, most of the black community were still experiencing a recession. When white America is in recession, black America is in an economic depression. Faced with the prospect of another recession, what the black community in such times need is what Asian, Jewish and White America has: an economically sound financial stimulus package not solely from government but much from their own established "Economic Sand Box", in other words a community group of financiers who lead the way of building an economically sound community within that will help average Asian, Jewish or White Americans with the most insecure jobs to remain economically strong as corporate entities and not company laborers. The lesson for the black community is this; the poorest among us are and will always be hurt by recessions, its design for the labor force. Stimulus proposals based on tax cuts for the wealthy or for business owners are not design to provide immediate relief to those of the poor still hurting from possible recession, much less protect the labor force from the additional damages continued recessions.

One approach to boost the economy was providing targeted supports through expanded unemployment insurance(social and domestic economic) and broad-based tax rebates, another was providing assistance to states to prevent tax increases or spending cuts, and directly stimulating job growth by accelerating funding for infrastructure and manufacturing particularity for bridge, school repair and automobile factories. It is always important to keep in mind that few black communities are better off than most and many are worse off. Frederick Douglass stated, back in the 1870s that "the Republican Party is the ship and all else is the storm" he summed up black America's rules of engagement with the nation's political and electoral apparatus. This was stated at a time doing the nineteenth century Democrats were the Confederate party, the party of secession and slavery, with whom no accommodation was possible. So as it was noted, the Republican party of that era was the ship, and all else the storm. But like many ships taken sail, this ship ride one did not sail in peaceful waters. Before Emancipation was a dozen years old, Northern white Republicans were washing their hands and looking the other way while Southern black Republican sheriffs, assessors, judges, county, state, federal legislators and other officials, were evicted from their posts amid hails of gunfire, white mob violence and ubiquitous threats. Republican voters in the South, mostly black, were driven from the polls by a reign of terror that robbed many of their lands and black businesses, thousands of mostly black lives loss, while white Northern Republicans averted their eyes and did nothing. But this betrayal failed to shake the rock solid political allegiance of most indigenous black families. For the most part, the Republican party was still the ship, and all else, the storm. Where and when they were allowed to vote at all, blacks continued to vote Republican. Over the next five decades, hundreds of thousands left Dixie for better opportunities throughout the north and west, where for the most part they remained Republicans. The Frederick Douglass strategy held sway over most of black politics till the Great Depression of the early 1930s, when black America finally jumped that Republican ship for the Democratic one. You'd think that many political leaders of that era might have negotiated properly.

They might have demanded voting rights for blacks in the solidly Democratic South, or perhaps a federal law against lynching in return for the black community allegiance it should be remembered that in the South and much of the rest of the country from the 1860s until the 1950s and 60s, white violence against black families went absolutely unpunished by local and federal law enforcement officials --- or at least open white opposition to Jim Crow on the part of Northern white Democrats. But sadly, they did not. When black America abandoned the Republican ship for the Democratic one in the 1930s, the black community got the same deal they had with the Republicans. The vote was kept outside the South, where it was already had. And now the Democratic Party was the designated ship, and all else the storm. It's been that way for decades, since anybody alive can remember. Although black America had switched parties, black America have carried Frederick Douglass's 1870 rules of engagement with the US political and electoral process into the 21st century, picking one of the two establishment political parties, and investing all energy, votes and political capital there, regardless of the result. It was simple, this was the "Making Of a Prosperous Slave Nation". Today so call black politicians still is channeling Frederick Douglass. The Democratic Party, in which they've invested their personal careers, 75 or 80 years of the black community votes and the energy of generations of volunteered labor remains the ship. All else is the storm. So the 1870 Frederick Douglass political strategy is still to this day working its way thru the black American community. Black folk in America to paraphrase an old principle, have no permanent friends or enemies, but our permanent foot print can be easily identified. These are labor force jobs, justice and injustice human rights at home, and peace abroad. Did such an 1870 political strategy deliver the black community jobs, justice and human rights at home, and peace abroad or just an injustice of life? Is American Colonial rule working for the black man and woman, if so, why is there a call to leave and why should we leave a land we established first. If it's not then maybe the question should be whether or not we're operating in the wrong position, or whether it's time to observe the wise operation of the white man and do likewise, as the Nation of Islam Leader Hon. Elijah Muhammad stated in the 1950.

Is the two parties political strategy delivering peace in the black community abroad? All of the permanent interests, jobs, justice, human rights and peace are all linked to colonial rule of life. America is a global empire, with 800 known military bases scattered around the world. There are no Turkish Air Force officers at corner bars in rural Alabama, or Chinese Marines with bases in Michigan, and you can't find Afghan or Nigerian sailors at any US port, unless your tax dollars are paying to train them. But there are uniformed US armed forces in 70 countries today. Dr. Martin Luther King Jr., pinpointed the war in Vietnam as the reason the 1960s War on Poverty programs could not be funded, funding the multiple wars needed to maintain and extend a global empire will absolutely prevent the funding of jobs, education, housing and health care for the foreseeable future of the black family. The Great Recession of 2007–2009 produced widespread unemployment for the black communities and some white families alike and so many had yet to overcome the still tentative economic recovery. All U.S. households were severely hurt by the recession but the black communities experienced a severe loss overall. That meant that, the economic recovery deepens and the labor market for the black communities had to climb out of a deeper hole to regain the same level of economic security as they had before the crisis. The level of economic security enjoyed by the black communities before the housing and financial crises drove the economy into the ditch was far lower than that of white families (though better than today's circumstances). The last business cycle, which lasted from the beginning of the last economic recession in March 2001 to the beginning of the Great Recession in December 2007, did little to close the economic gap between the black communities and whites in some cases even exacerbated the difference in economic security. The Great Recession thus made a bad situation worse. Many communities, particularly Black and Latinos, experienced similar hardships during this recession even though their experience during the preceding business cycle varied substantially. Black America saw few economic gains during that days business cycle, with stagnant or declining homeownership and wages, high unemployment rates, and low employment rates even as the economy grew.

Latinos, in comparison, saw comparatively strong jobs gains that were reflected in other gains, particularly in homeownership, during that times business cycle. The gains were insufficient to provide any buffer for Latinos once the recession hit, leading Latinos to lose most of the ground gained during that previous times business cycle. Much of the data shown at that time that Asian Americas' employment and earnings are generally on par with those of whites, but the data was dominated by Chinese and Indian Americas as well. Other Asian nationalities, among them Vietnamese Americans and Cambodian Americans, were struggling to recover from the Great Recession, but limited data disguise the diversity within the Asian-Americas community and not showing much of the Jewish American community, I wonder why?. Still, even the existing data at the time for Asian Americas showed substantial economic struggles in the worst recession alongside economic hardships for white families. The diverse consequences of the Great Recession and the ensuing recovery for the black communities in this nation was clear evidence in different sets of data. Specifically the data had shown:

- Substantial differences in economic security that exist by race and ethnicity. The unemployment rate for blacks, for instance, was 15.8 percent in the fourth quarter of 2010, compared to 12.9 percent for Latinos, 7.3 percent for Asian Americas, and 8.7 percent for whites.
- Homeownership rates tell a similar story. In the third quarter of 2010, the homeownership rate for Black Americas was 45.0 percent. The homeownership rate for Latinos was 47.0 percent, and the homeownership rate for whites was 74.7 percent.
- Racial and ethnic differences had worsened or stayed the same during the recession and recovery. Unemployment rates rose faster for Blacks and Latinos than for whites while homeownership rates fell faster. Trends for poverty rates, health insurance coverage, and retirement savings also show widening gaps by race and ethnicity throughout the recession and recovery after 2007.

Economic security losses during the recession and recovery exacerbated the already weak situation for blacks. They experienced declining employment rates, rising poverty rates, falling homeownership rates, decreasing health insurance and low company retirement coverage during the cycle from 2001 to 2007.

- The recession and recovery quickly eliminated the modest gains that Latinos had seen during that business cycle. Latino homeownership rates in 2010, were close to their levels in 2001 even though Latino
- homeownership rates had risen from 2000 to 2007.

The main lessons from this data were threefold. First, all families struggled with the prolonged economic and labor market slumps, regardless of race or ethnicity. Second, economic differences by race and ethnicity remained intact during the crisis, meaning that the black communities went into a deeper economic hole than whites. Third, the economic downturn quickly translated into a lot of economic pain for the black communities since they had seen few gains, either with respect to jobs, earnings, or both, during that times preceding business cycle. The data suggested that the black communities had faced continued structural obstacles to gain the same economic opportunities as white families, even during good economic times. This implied three policy lessons some policymakers(colonial rule of life in America) needed to pay continued attention to the weak labor market to ensure there is a rising tide that can lift all boats. Policies that intended to create more jobs needed to include provisions that particularly target the black communities. Third, policymakers needed to put in place policies that could go beyond the immediate need for job creation for everybody to help erase differences in economic security and opportunity by race(in front). The unemployment rate is always one of the most fundamental tools to understanding the overall health of the labor market. At the end of 2010, the unemployment rate for Blacks and Latinos remained considerably higher than that of white, Asian and Jewish Americans. In the fourth quarter of 2010, the unemployment rate for European Americans was 8.7 percent, while the unemployment rate for Asian Americas was much lower at 7.3 percent. Comparably, the unemployment rates for Blacks and Latinos at the end of 2010 were 15.8 percent and 12.9 percent. In December 2007, the start of the last recession, the quarterly unemployment rate for whites was 4.2 percent or 4.5 percentage points less than three years later. Similarly, the unemployment rate for Asian Americans was 3.7 percent or percentage points lower than at the end of 2010.

The unemployment rate for Blacks was 8.6 percent in December 2007, or 7.2 percentage points lower than in December 2010. And the unemployment rate for Latinos had increased by 7.1 percentage points by December 2010 from a level of 5.8 percent in December 2007. The increases in the unemployment rate over the past three years started from higher levels for colored folk than for whites and they rose much faster for the blacks than for whites. The unemployment rate for blacks was 8.1 percent in March 2001 and the unemployment rate for Latinos was 6.0 percent, compared to 3.4 percent for Asian Americans and percent for whites. These gaps remained by December 2007, which meant that the black communities entered the most severe recession since the Great Depression from a position of relative economic weakness compared to that of whites and some parts of the Asian- American community. These structural differences in unemployment rates by race and ethnicity meant that the black communities fell into a deeper hole in terms of economic security during the recession. Blacks were in more desperate need of policy attention to jobs, wages, and benefits than whites to just recover the losses they suffered during the recession since they experienced sharper economic security losses. Black people typically don't want to be unemployed. They are prone and designed to think job. An indicator of the employment opportunities for the black community is the employment-to-population ratio, which shows the share of people in a community who have a job. A higher number suggests more job opportunities and a lower number indicates fewer job opportunities. And a decline in the employment-to-population ratio means that job growth is not keeping up with population growth, while an increase in the employment-to-population ratio shows that job growth outpaces population growth. The employment-to-population ratio measures how well employment gains and losses are keeping up with population changes. The employed share of the population for whites stood at 59.1 percent in the last quarter of 2010, compared to 58.4 percent for Latinos, 59.9 percent for Asian Americas, and 52.4 percent for Blacks. Employment opportunities were especially hard to come by for Black folks three years into the business cycle that started in December 2007. Employment opportunities disappeared more quickly for black communities than for whites over the past three years.

The percent of whites with a job dropped 4.4 percentage points since the start of the recession, while the rate for Latinos declined 6.1 percentage points, for Black folks fell by 5.4 percentage points, and for Asian Americas decreased by 4.4 percentage points. The decline in the employment-to-population ratios for all population groups indicates that job growth has fallen well below population growth over the past three years, more so for Blacks and Latinos than for others. These current figures are a marked decline from where they were in March 2001 when that last business cycle began. At that point, 64.9 percent of white Americans and 65.9 percent of Latinos were employed, 65.3 percent of Asian Americas had jobs, and 60.5 percent of Black Americas found work.   The struggles of the black communities are even more when examining how well actual employment levels live up to the employment levels, relative to the respective populations, at the end of 2007. This comparison gives a sense of how deep the jobs whole currently is for the black population. By comparing current employment to pre-recession employment we can engage how much damage the 2007 recession did to black employment prospects. At the end of 2010, white Americans' actual employment level was 93.4 percent of their pre-recession employment level, meaning that employment was almost seven percent below where it needed to be to put whites just back to where they were at the start of the recession. For Asian Americans that number was 93.1 percent, for African Americans it was 90.7 percent, and for Latinos it was 90.8 percent. Blacks and Latinos were thus in a much deeper employment hole by the fourth quarter of 2010 compared to the start of the recession in December 2007. The business cycle, though, was already marked by weak employment growth. Job growth fell behind population growth for almost all groups, even before the Great Recession hit. The employment-to-population ratio for whites declined by an average annual rate of 0.2 percentage points per year between March 2001 and December 2007, while the ratio declined by an average annual rate of 0.4 percentage points for Black Americas, 0.1 percentage points for Asian Americas, and 0.2 percentage points for Latinos. These employment data showed two crucial points. First, all population groups were in a weaker economic position at the end of that business cycle (December 2007) than at the beginning of that business cycle (March 2001).

So during an economic upturn they experienced an erosion of economic prosperity. Second, economic security declined more sharply for Black Americas and Latinos, and possibly for some parts of the Asian-Americas community, than for whites. As the economy struggles, increased part-time employment rates indicate the severity of economic hardships for families across the country. Many job seekers thus turn to part-time employment to at least have a job. The important indicator for the weakness in the labor market is the change in the share of people working part time, since other social, cultural, and economic factors can determine the level of part-time employment. In the fourth quarter of 2010, 15.5 percent of Black Americas, 16.9 percent of Latinos, 15.6 percent of Asian Americas, and 18.6 percent of whites worked fewer than 35 hours each week. These levels mirrored much larger increases in part-time employment for the black communities than for whites. Black Americas and Latinos have seen more significant increases in part-time employment compared to whites and Asian Americas. The share of Asian Americas working part time has gone up by 2.1 percentage points over the past three years, while the share of part-time workers has increased 1.7 percentage points in the same period. The numbers again show faster increases in economic weaknesses for black communities than for whites since their shares of part-time workers have risen faster than was the case for whites. People not only seek a job but also a job that pays well enough to make ends meet. Median weekly earnings—defined as half of all households with incomes that are above the median and the other half with incomes below the median—shed some light on the quality of jobs that Americans hold. The numbers indicate that Latinos and blacks continue to hold lower- quality jobs relative to their white and Asian-American counterparts as they typically earn significantly less money per week. As of the third quarter of 2010, the period for which this data details, African Americans' usual median weekly earnings were $623 in 2009 dollars and Latinos earned $532. In comparison, whites made $774 each week, while Asians earned $871. This earnings gap is nothing new. Throughout the decade, Blacks and Latinos have consistently brought home less money each week compared to whites. At the beginning of the business cycle of March 2001, whites' median usual weekly earnings stood at $731.

Blacks earned $582 weekly, or 79.7 percent of what whites did, while Latinos earned $493 weekly, or 67. 4 percent of what whites made on average. By the end of the business cycle in December 2007, Blacks earned, on average, about 82.8 percent of what whites earned, and Latinos earned 73.1 percent of what whites did. This suggests that, despite a slight narrowing, large earnings gaps persisted at the start of the Great Recession. These gaps widened as the economy began to recover from the recession. In the third quarter of 2010, Blacks and Latino families earned 80.5 percent and 68.8 percent of what whites made, respectively. Communities of color thus not only saw job opportunities disappear more quickly than was the case for whites, but the quality of their jobs also fell more during the recession than was the case for whites. Household income statistics provide the most comprehensive measure of the current economic resources that households have available. In addition to wages, household income incorporates other forms of revenue received, such as unemployment insurance, child support payments, social security, and rental income. The data report the median household income, which is the income level that splits all households into two equal groups—half of all households have incomes that are above the median and the other half have incomes below the median. In 2009, the available data showed, median household incomes were substantially lower for the black communities than for whites. The median household income of the black community was $32,584 in 2009 dollars, more than 40 percent less than that of whites, who earned $54,461. And Latinos had a median income of $34,088, or about 30 percent below that of whites in 2009. Asian Americans had a median income of $65,469 in 2009, which was about 20 percent higher than that of whites. All groups saw sharp income decreases during the Great Recession. The median income of whites fell by $2,353 from 2007 to 2009 in 2009 dollars; the median income of Asian Americans dropped by $2,913; the median income of African Americans decreased by $2,502; and the median income of Latinos dropped by $1,974. In relative terms, this meant a decrease of 4.1 percent for whites, 4.3 percent for Asian Americans, 4.9 percent for Latinos, and 7.1 percent for African Americans. The data showed a sharper erosion of economic security for the black communities than for whites. The decreases during the recession continued the trend from the last business cycle, when median incomes also declined. On the whole, incomes have declined across the board this decade.

African Americans and Latinos were hit the hardest. Since 2000, African Americans' household incomes decreased 1.4 percent per year, while the median income for Latinos declined 0.9 percent annually. These rates are significantly higher than that of whites, whose incomes declined 0.5 percent per year, and for Asian Americans, whose median income dropped by 0.7percent each year between 2000 and 2009. Combined with the fact that Black Americas and Latino household incomes started the decade lagging behind those of whites, the steady decrease in house- hold income at accelerated rates only serves to widen the earnings gap. The percentage of the U.S. population living below the poverty line increased for all racial groups in the recession, more so for communities of color than for whites. In 2009, more than one in four Latino (25.3 percent) and Black Americas families (25.8 percent) lived below the poverty line. Conversely, poverty rates among white Americans and Asian Americas were 9.4 percent and 12.5 percent, respectively. These figures show more pronounced increases in the poverty rates for communities of color than for whites during the recession. The poverty rate increased by 1.3 percentage points for African Americans, by 3.8 percentage points for Latinos, and by 2.3 percentage points for Asian Americas from 2007 to 2009. The comparable increase for whites was 1.2 percentage points during that period. These increases in the poverty rate followed a worsening or unchanged poverty situation for all groups. In 2000, the poverty rate among African Americans was 22.5 percent, rising to 24.5 percent in 2007. For Latinos the poverty rate in 2000 was 21.5 percent, the same as in 2007. The poverty rate for Asian Americas in 2007 was 10.2 percent, rising from 9.9 percent in 2000, and the poverty rate for whites increased from 7.4 percent in 2000 to 8.2 percent in 2007. All groups saw rising poverty throughout the past nine years. These increases, though, occurred from much higher levels of poverty for minorities than for whites, exacerbating severe economic security in communities of color. Health insurance provides access to medical care. The cost of coverage is often prohibitive, and coverage rates reflect the economic well-being of families across the country. In 2009 (the last year with available data), 12.0 percent of white Americans lacked health insurance. The number of uninsured African Americans was 9.0 percent higher than white Americans in 2009, with 21.0 percent. Latinos had the largest share of uninsured people with 32.4 percent in 2009. And 17.2 percent of Asian Americans lacked health insurance in 2009.

The black communities were clearly a lot more economically insecure than whites. The share of people without health insurance increased in all groups during the recession. The share rose by 1.6 percentage points from 10.4 percent in 2007 for whites, by 1.5 percentage points from 19.5 percent for African Americans, by 0.3 percentage points from 32.1 percent for Latinos, and by 0.7 percentage points from 16.8 percent for Asian Americas. These increases reversed the improvements of health insurance coverage for some groups while exacerbating the losses during the last business cycle for others. The share of whites without health insurance rose from 9.1 percent to 10.4 percent between 2000 and 2007 and from 18.3 percent to 19.5 percent for Black Americas. The shares, though, fell from 32.6 percent to 32.1 percent for Latinos and from 17.5 percent to 16.8 percent for Asian Americas. Most of these meager gains were erased in the recession that followed. The gap between white and nonwhite homeownership rates remains significant at the end of the decade. As of the third quarter of 2010, the homeownership rate was 74.7 percent for whites, while only 47.0 percent of Latinos were homeowners. The homeownership rate for Black Americas was 45.0 percent. These data show declining homeownership rates for communities of color and rising rates for whites during the recession. The white homeownership rate fell by 0.2 percentage points from 2007 to the third quarter of 2010. The African-American homeownership rate fell by 2.7 percentage points from 47.7 percent to 45.0 percent, and the Latino homeownership rate decreased by 1.5 percentage points from 48.5 percent in December 2007 to 47.0 percent in the third quarter of 2010. In the previous business cycle, whites and Latinos saw increased homeownership rates while Black Americas did not. From 2001 to 2007, the homeownership rate for whites increased 1.2 percent, from 74.3 percent in 2001 to 75.2 percent in 2007. The homeownership rate for Latinos rose a whopping 5.1 percent in that last business cycle. Their overall homeownership rose to 49.7 percent in 2007 from 47.3 percent in 2001.Black Americas homeownership rates declined in the same time period, dropping 1.1 percent from 2001 to 2007. The Black Americas homeownership rate was 47.7 percent in 2001 and 46.2 percent in 2007. The decline in the Black Americas homeownership rate from 2001 to 2007 only exacerbated their struggles in the recession. Foreclosure rates provided some insight as to how well black communities were faring in the financial and economic crisis.

The foreclosure rate on loans issued between 2005 and 2008 was 4.52 percent for whites. For Asian Americas, the rate was 4.60 percent. Latinos and Black Americas had significantly higher foreclosure rates, at 7.69 percent for Latinos and 7.90 percent for Black Americas. When controlling for income, disparities still exist today, especially for Black Americas. Among low-income Americans of all groups, Black Americas received 14.8 percent of loans but made up 21.0 percent of the foreclosures. Among middle-income Americans, Black Americas received 12.3 percent of all loans but are 18.0 percent of the foreclosures. Even among those with high incomes, Black Americas constituted a disproportionate share of all foreclosures. The picture the same for Latinos. In all income categories, the shares of Latino homeowners in foreclosures outnumber their share of total loans, although the differences to whites were not quite as stark as for Black Americans. Similar, planning and saving for retirement placed financial burdens on families. The percentage of individuals with employer-based retirement plans from the private sector declined across the board in 2008. Less than half of Black Americas—45.6 percent—had access to employer-based retirement savings, down 1.5 percentage points from 2007. Less than a third of Hispanics—30.3 percent—had employer-based retirement plans, down 0.3 percentage points from 2007. Whites also saw a decline, with only 56.6 percent having employer-based retirement plans, down one percentage point from the year before that. Access to employer-based retirement plans has slowly declined since 2002, the earliest this data was available. The percentage of Black Americas with these plans had declined 0.3 percentage points annually, while the percentage of whites with these plans had declined 0.2 percent annually. Hispanics had the lowest of access to such plans, but their decline since 2002 had been slower—0.1 percentage points a year. Communities of color face ongoing systematic economic inequalities in the 21st century. Though many have been remedied by progressive policymaking and community-conscientious practices, much is left to do to equalize the economic tide for the black communities. The key policy recommendations came from a Center's Progress 2050 project that would help alleviate many of these inequalities. Unemployment benefits provided much-needed assistance to unemployed individuals and their families while they work to find a new job.

Unemployment insurance is especially important for the black communities because they face higher levels of unemployment and significantly lack of wealth, but it's also the black communities Achilles Heel as well. The source and reasons for these disparities are well-documented but the bottom line is that unemployment insurance would provide critical assistance to unemployed individuals and their families while they find a new job and would enable those out of work to keep putting food on the table and pay their bills. Moreover, there's a strong economic case for continuing these benefits. Unemployment benefits are one of the most effective and efficient ways to boost demand, which is what many economy needs. Economists estimate that the economy grows by $1.61 for every dollar spent on unemployment benefits because recipients typically spend all of their benefit payments quickly. A return to a noncontroversial, nonexpendable perception of unemployment insurance is critical for communities where so many are vulnerable to the racial wealth gap and long-term job seeking. If we do not ensure the long-term sound economic for our community viability of unemployment benefits, will continue to flourish in the forms of chronic debt, lower asset holdings and patterned economic deficits for the black communities became a detriment impact toward the nation's economy overall. Many immigrant workers, particularly those who are unauthorized, tend to be concentrated in the lowest-wage occupations, enduring very low wages in order to avoid being fired or, worse yet, deported. When immigrant labor is fully exploited all workers suffer. Immigration reform would build real economic security for workers, both U.S. and foreign born, as it would protect all workers rights to fair working conditions, protection from discrimination, and the right to organize for fair pay and benefits. The equitable immigration reform practice ensures that unscrupulous employer practices are not encouraged by lowered standards industry wide or unethical occupational demands made of immigrant employees. Operational practices that has undermine all workers rights as well as many being prohibited by comprehensive reform. Comprehensive immigration reform would also lead to increasing economic stability at the national level. According to a recent study, legalization would generate an estimated $2 trillion in cumulative gross domestic product over 5 or 10 years after its implementation—such that the number and quality of good jobs for all workers would increase.

In addition, immigration reform provides better jobs for all workers by improving industry standards in wages, safety, and benefits. Absent a body of exploitable workers subject to the most dangerous, low-paid, and physically demanding of jobs, all employees can experience a raised economic floor that ensures competitive wages and benefits for job seekers. Quality jobs are, at a minimum, defined as paying a wage that can support a family, provide health insurance, and assure retirement benefits. As recovery from the national economic crisis calls often and for jobs, often times the necessary quality jobs falls by the wayside. A 2008 analysis from the Economic Policy Institute indicated that 31.5 percent of white American workers had good jobs that could support a family, provided health insurance, and assured retirement benefits. Latinos had less than half of that percentage with only 14.4 percent occupying good jobs, while 21.8 percent of all black workers and 28.1 percent of Asian workers lagged behind, with quality jobs that made enough wages to support a family and received essential benefits. These stats are evidence that it is essential to bring the focus to quality jobs amid an economic recovery. Quality jobs can be promoted by increasing incentives for employers in the food and service industry to offer employees living wages and benefits above the minimum standard; mandating publicly subsidized development projects; and employers that receive broadly defined business assistance to provide living wages that will create stable employment opportunities and increased access to benefits for lower-wage workers. With these quality employment standards in place, the economic floor can realistically be raised for all employees and employers. The case for good jobs is unequivocal to create entrepreneurship as well . Analysis of the American Community Survey shows that unmarried black women make the least in comparison to all other groups of people. Gendered pay inequalities create a great deal of black women economic vulnerabilities. On average, women earn 77 cents for every dollar men make. White women earn roughly 79 cents per white male dollar. In 2009, Latinas earned only 76 percent of white women's median weekly full-time employment earnings, or roughly 60 cents for every dollar earned by a white man. Paycheck fairness matters greatly for black folk as gendered disparities in pay reduce the overall assets of families and communities with less accumulated wealth and substantial dependence upon women's wage earnings.

A comprehensive paycheck fairness bill that legislates away the gender pay gap will dramatically improve the economic well-being for economically sound communities that largely depend upon the financial contributions of women. A legislative sweep for women's equal pay will give black women an immediate economic boost. The continued implementation of tax credits that extend economic support for the country's lowest-earning households is always welcomed news. Yet the Making Work Pay credit, a $400 flat credit for tax filers written into the American Recovery and Reinvestment Act, was allowed to expire at the end of 2010. As a result, 25 million low-wage workers faced a tax hike. The Tax Relief bill switched Making Work Pay out for a 2 percent cut on the Social Security payroll tax, which means each taxpayer pockets 2 percent more of their paycheck for two years. But for single people earning less than $20,000 a year, the lowest-income earners of all, they would actually see less tax return than had the Making Work Pay credit remained in place resulting in a tax increase. As an alternative a strong recommendation that a federally implemented stop-gap credit would easily remedy this tax burden. The   stop-gap   credit   would make up the difference between the expired $400 Making Work Pay credit and the 2 percent Social Security payroll tax cut. This step would have provide tax equality for all taxpayers, both low income and rich. This stop-gap credit could have been implemented for even less than one-tenth of the cost of extending bonus Bush tax   cuts   for   the wealthiest Americans at the time for those that need the least economic Homeownership, continued to represent an important wealth-building lever for low-income households and homebuyers . For low-income communities, the loss of wealth to foreclosure was devastating. The Center for Responsible Lending analyzed the demographics of the foreclosure crisis in 2010 found that nearly 8 percent of both African Americans and Latinos have lost their homes to foreclosures, compared to 4.5 percent of whites. Furthermore, a home owned by a black family was found to be 76 percent more likely to go through foreclosure than a home owned by a white family. Easing constraints to homeownership in a way that protected against the risk of default through malicious nonbank lending practices was critical to addressing the concurrent racial homeownership and wealth gaps.

Knowing that black homebuyers were more likely to receive high-interest loans than white homebuyers—even when controlling for legitimate risk factors such as credit worthiness—consumer protection practices in the mortgage market are imperative. Included was state-endorsed consumer protection practices that ensured brokers acts in the interest of borrowers, circumscribing the practice of steering subprime loans to buyers who would qualify for prime loans. Consumer-oriented practices that would support black homebuyers safely entering the market also include the; promotion of homebuyer education, loan counseling, and direct grants to offset cash-at-closing costs. To help them stay in the market, state regulations of both loan refinancing and mandatory mediation before foreclosure were recommended best practices for fair lending. A report from Nielsen, "The Increasingly Affluent, Educated and Diverse," explored the "untold story" of African-American consumers, Black households earning $75,000 or more per year. According to the report at the time, Black people in this segment were growing faster in size and influence than whites in all income groups above $60,000. And as African-American incomes increased, their spending surpasses that of the total population in areas such as insurance policies, pensions and retirement savings. "These larger incomes were attributed to a number of factors, including youthfulness, immigration, advanced educational attainment and increased digital acumen. As these factors changed African-Americans' decisions as brand loyalists and ambassadors, savvy marketers were taking notice," according to Cheryl Pearson-McNeil, Senior Vice President U.S. Strategic Community Alliances and Consumer Engagement and Saul Rosenberg, Chief Content Officer at Nielsen. It was projected that by 2060, the Black population will increase from 45.7 million to 74.5 million, with 17.9 percent of the U.S. population. From 2000 to 2014, the rate of Black American population growth was more than double that of the white rate of 8.2 percent, and 35 percent faster than the U.S. population as a whole. According to Nielsen at that time, the "youthfulness and vitality" among Black consumers were being driven by a diverse influx of immigrants, who made up one in 11 Black Americas, or 8.7 percent.

There has been a substantial education growth among Blacks, with high school graduation rates exceeding 70 percent, outpacing the growth for all students nationwide. In addition, Blacks are making gains in STEM (science, technology, engineering and mathematics) careers, helping to fuel income gains. The largest increase for Black households was in the number of households making over $200,000, an increase of 138 percent compared to a total population increase of 74 percent. "The year 2015 represented a tipping point for Black Americas. As media consumers, powerful cultural influencers experiencing population growth created an unprecedented impact across a broad range of industries, in television, music, social media and social issues," according to a report. Black consumers were digitally empowered and well-versed in social media, helping to shape and shift the national discourse. And Black people are youthful — with an average age of 31.4 as opposed to 39 for whites and 36.7 for the total population and rising in cultural influence, driving mainstream trends in music, television, music and other areas. Therefore, a report notes, those who market to Millennial and young people must reach Black youth. Other results of this report include evidence of strong Black growth among income earners above $100,000 in metro areas of the South, such as Augusta and Columbus, Georgia; Baton Rouge, Louisiana; and Aiken, South Carolina. The report also found that gatherings, festivals, reunions and other social events are popular among African-Americans. Black buying trends show an emphasis on family and cooking ingredients tied to cultural traditions, and an expectation that the brands they buy will support social causes. According to the report "Black American households spend more on basic food ingredients and beverages and tend to value the food preparation process, spending more time than average preparing meals. Other popular buying categories include fragrances, personal health and beauty products, as well as family planning, household cleaning products." The report emphasizes that as the social and cultural clout of the Black consumer is on the ascendancy, it is incumbent upon advertisers and marketers of consumer brands to develop a long-term economic spending game with the Black community. As noted, Black buying power has to reached $1.5 trillion and $1.8 trillion by 2021, according to the University of Georgia's Selig Center for Economic Growth, other reports vary in numbers.

That is so much combined spending power that it would make Black America the 13th largest economy in the world in terms of Gross Domestic Product, the size of Russia based on World Bank data. By comparison, in 1990, Black buying power was $320 billion. As the largest consumer group of color, in a nation that is becoming increasingly darker, this trend will only continue to have its impact on the U.S. But in the end what does all of this really mean? We know that the Black community has much money at its disposal. What is the end goal for Black consumers, to merely buy more "stuff" that depletes in value and gets us nowhere, or rather to invest, own and build our community with full wealth? As corporate America and the business community vie for the patronage of the African-American community, Black dollars must serve as leverage to become its own corporate community. Black consumers must use their resources wisely for purposes to reward family, friends & neighbors and punish foes accordingly, supporting and building up Black-owned business and those brands that are in sync within interests, values and aspirations. People and forces outside of the community want black business, but many will do little to nothing for it, or more importantly, for the black community, with no investments in the community and no jobs as well. Consider the companies that spend billions of dollars every year on advertising, but less than 3% of that went to Black publications, Black TV and radio stations and the casting of Black actors, as it has been in the Marketplace. America is a highly developed mixed economy. It is the world's largest economy by nominal GDP; it is also the second largest by purchasing power parity (PPP), behind China. It has the world's sixth highest per capita GDP (nominal) and the eighth highest per capita GDP (PPP) as of 2024. The U.S. accounted for 26% of the global economy in 2023 in nominal terms, and about 15.5% in PPP terms. The U.S. dollar is the currency of record most used in international transactions and is the world's reserve currency, backed by a large U.S. treasuries market, its role as the reference standard for the petrodollar system, and its linked euro-dollar. Several countries use it as their official currency and in others it is the de facto currency. Since the end of World War II, the economy has achieved relatively steady growth, low unemployment and inflation, and rapid advances in technology. The American economy is fueled by high productivity, well developed transportation infrastructure, and extensive natural resources. Americans have the sixth highest average household and employee income among OECD member states. In 2021, they had the highest median household income.

The Worlds 13th Wealthiest Nation

The U.S. has one of the world's highest income inequalities among the developed countries. The largest U.S. trading partners are Canada, Mexico, China, Japan, Germany, South Korea, the United Kingdom, Taiwan, India, and Vietnam. The U.S. is the world's largest importer and second largest exporter. It has free trade agreements with several countries, including Canada and Mexico through the USMCA (United State, Mexico, Canada Agreement) Australia, South Korea, Israel, and several others that are in effect or under negotiation. The U.S. has a highly flexible labor market, where the industry adheres to a hire-and-fire policy, and job security is relatively low. Among OECD nations, the U.S. has a highly efficient and strong social security system; social expenditure stood at roughly 30% of GDP. The United States is the world's largest producer of petroleum and natural gas. In 2016, it was the world's largest trading country and second largest manufacturer, with American manufacturing making up a fifth of the global total. The U.S. not only has the largest internal market for goods, but also dominates the services trade. Total U.S. trade was $4.2 trillion in 2018. The world's largest companies(500) 121 are headquartered in the U.S. alone, The U.S. has the world's highest number of billionaires, with total wealth of $3.0 trillion. U.S. commercial banks had $22.9 trillion in assets in December 2022. U.S. global assets under management had more than $30 trillion in assets. During the Great Recession of 2008, the U.S. economy suffered a significant decline. The American Reinvestment and Recovery Act was enacted by the United States Congress, and in the ensuing years the U.S. experienced the longest economic expansion on record by July 2019. The New York Stock Exchange and Nasdaq are the world's largest stock exchanges by market capitalization and trade volume. The U.S. has the world's largest gold reserve, with over 8,000 tons of gold. In 2014, the U.S. economy was ranked first in international ranking on venture capital and global research and development funding. The U.S. spends around 3.46% of GDP on cutting-edge research and development across various sectors of the economy. The U.S. has produced the world's highest number of Nobel laureates in the economics field. It is also the world's fourth largest high-technology exporter. The U.S. ranks second in the world by number of patent applications.

Consumer spending comprised 68% of the U.S. economy in 2022, while its labor share of income was 44% in 2021.The U.S. has the world's largest consumer market.[87] The nation's labor market has attracted immigrants from all over the world and its net migration rate is among the highest in the world. The U.S. is one of the top-performing economies in studies such as the Ease of Doing Business Index, the Global Competitiveness Report, and others. And yet, Black folks don't have jobs simply because of not establishing their gift of entrepreneurship in their communities as our ethnic counter groups. For all of this wealth, it doesn't feel like wealth because of heavy duty spending of all moneys outside the Black community. As a black scholar noted we need to harness that wealth. He said that with over $1 trillion, one can buy: 1,000 NFL teams; 3,000 predominantly white universities; the annual budget of 1.4 million charter schools across the nation; pay the tuition at Howard University for 50 million students for an entire year; buy 854,000 community centers; purchase NBC, ESPN and CBS and still have $1 trillion left over. "When you look at Black unemployment, you see that Black unemployment is typically 2 to 3 times as high as white unemployment," He said. "Ask yourself this: Why is it that we give away $1.5 trillion in spending power when that $1.5 trillion could, according to most economists,   create 15 million jobs in the Black community?" He added: "So, the point of all of this, the reason I'm telling you all of this, He says, is because one have to understand one important, fundamental fact. That your money is your power, and you cannot give your power away." Furthermore, Black consumers are not respected, they continue to face institutional racism, policies that undermine their families, severe police harassment tactics and mass incarceration." If Black Lives Matter, it also must matter to the Black Community as well and that we can no longer pay good money to finance our own economic depression. Martin Luther King Jr. along with others did right with the Montgomery Bus Boycott, the Black Community was severely disrespected, many forced to sit in the back of the bus. Adam Clayton Powell led his own bus boycott in New York because the Transit Authority did not hire black folk, and he was involved in the struggles against Harlem Hospital, Harlem drug stores, and other businesses that refused to hire Black folk.

This is what economic boycotts and disinvestment in apartheid days of South Africa was all about. A local newspaper company out of Philly once reported, there is a new movement to economically empower the Black community throughout the country. LetsBuyBlack365 was a national grassroots movement that was to utilizes the online community and local networking to harness Black buying power, with a goal to create jobs and resources to help Black people. The organization's had videos to tell all there is to know. A spokeswoman for the group, spoke to a newspaper that, quote, "this is a critical time for their efforts, as Black people watch with dismay as Black people are killed by police and the offending officers are not indicted". "What stood out most was that these things don't happen in communities where they have political power. Political power comes from having economic power, through having businesses that can lobby and represent their interests," she said. "It puts empowerment on the individual to say, 'what can I do right now? I can't do anything about the demise of Sandra Bland, I can't do anything about some of these other people but I can do something about political power in order to have some sort of social justice for the future,'" she added. "If our communities are to change economically, it is going to be up to the black community and business leaders to lead the charge" as quoted. We can help win the war on poverty in our communities," Simply by forming a purchase power agreement with black businesses. Our black businesses must figure out how to grow as one entity for purpose of hiring more of our people from out of own communities. We must be able to train our people from our own community corporate business ethics so they would be able to lead productive lives. It is important to create a foundation that is sustainable and improve the state of the Indigenous Black Family in America. GOD did not intend for us as a people to live in such high level of poverty. We are a highly spiritually connected people of GOD, but yet we live a disconnected life of GOD and if you are disconnected from GOD you can only be connected to another source of defeated power called devil. There is no neutral zone between the Kingdom of GOD and the Kingdom of Devil. You are either in devil's kingdom or GOD's Kingdom, either way you become an enemy to both. If I am to be an enemy to one's kingdom I'd rather be an enemy to devil's kingdom than an enemy to "The Kingdom Of GOD".

Proper management of our black communities money to create an agenda and move our people forward — that's been the goal since the days of the 60s. In many areas of our black community there are too many layers of distrust amongst us which prevent us from moving forward as a collective unit. It's a result of living in America, where we've been systematically oppressed in every aspect of our existence in this land called America, severely divided by negatively mentally manipulated not to be a unified black community. Surely, we have a lot to heal from dealing with our past history of things but GOD is bigger than our last experiences. We must fight as our lives depend on it, for our future generations to come as time continues to press forward. So many black lives are being sacrificed by way of an ethnic purge, being carried out by a 1950 mindset of white men and women law of enforcement. This 1950 mindset of white folk are afraid of the loss of their 62% white privilege majority people power only in America. A continued lack of unification will remain to be an extremely difficult process of life for our community abroad. It's a process we must not continue in order to change the outcomes for our communities today and our communities in the future times to come. The Elite Societies in the United States of America only recognize the economically sound communities such as Asians, Jewish and Anglo-Saxons of America. There is one black community the elites of America respects and honor quietly and that is the "Nation Of Islam", Why? because this black community under the leadership of now Hon. Min. Louis Farrakhan knows how things work in American Elite Society. One way of knowing is thru the former Head of the Nation the Hon. Elijah Muhammad, stating in the 1950s....quote..."Observe the wise operation of the white man and do likewise". A message of instructions to which he passed down to his people of this great black community to follow and apply to their lives and you can today see the results of this powerful instructions. There is nothing in any rule book that says you can't unify, there is nothing in any rule book that says you can't succeed. But there are many people, places and things that you allow to stop you from reaching these highest heights. Why so? Because one spirit entity that knows the desire of your heart is devil. Devil reads your playbook of how you live, devil study you and I day & night.

This practice is what keeps devil a step ahead of our lifestyle every day and every day as we awaken in our day, devil already planted his people in place to attack and distract you and I from applying the number one basic principle of life called "DISCIPLINE". We as a people must master discipline in our decision making process. We must discipline in this area of our thinking because our thinking process is the battle ground of the spiritual warfare that is at hand every day, all day around us. In other words whoever controls the mind controls the body and the human mind is the battle ground that devil fights to co-habit and controls by way of a manipulative method called "A STRONGHOLD". Any lifestyle desire devil has studied of you and I he then take that lifestyle desire and use it in a manipulative stronghold method that will immediately lock your thinking process into a stronghold thought process that leads to his control over the mind and body. Once in his control you find yourself doing all things that you are not supposed to be doing and none of the things you were designed and intended to do. The 14% black community is the only community in America that has a 1.5 trillion dollar spending habit, with no political power, no voice of power, no discipline economic power, but yet holds the 13 wealthiest position as a nation being in the top GNI rating in the world's economy. What is the magic wand for our people to know their position in the world? What will it take to gather our people in a unified manner to take up our true position in the world? Why are we a people so blind to our own economically sound position in the world, let alone in America? How many black folk has to die before many black folk can live in their true position in the world? How many more black men has to either continue to be systematically separated from their black woman and children or choose to walk away from their families? How many more black woman has to choose their career over a strong relationship that leads to marriage with the black man? How many more black children must learn to live a grown man and woman life long before their time? How many more black leaders, pastor, preacher, teachers are allowed to abuse their position of power & authority? How many more black churches will become black circuses? How many more black men must die at the hands of a racist white man or woman officer? When do the black community awaken to a day of honor & respect for being a recognized economically sound community, that's well respected in America and the world? These kind of questions must be answered for a final time.

Why? because our time is running out. Today, the Black community faces a serious irony. Little more than 50 years ago, Black communities wanted Black men to protect them from White men who wore "hoods" while they killed Black people and destroyed their property. Fifty years later, Black communities are asking local (mostly White) police departments and state National Guard units to protect them from our sons and neighbors: mostly young Black men in "hoodies" and ski masks who are killing Black people and destroying their property. Whether perpetrated by the Ku Klux Klan or by young Black men this terrorism is decimating Black communities. Opportunities for positive community development and growth are smothered when young Black men murder other young Black men and inadvertently maim and kill other innocent people in these communities. Children are afraid to travel to and from school, middle-income Blacks refuse to reside in high-crime communities, business owners steer clear of inner-city areas and senior citizens become easy prey. Black communities become paralyzed and implode under the weight of Black-on-Black crime, violence and murder. Five strategies, outlined by the U.S. Centers for Disease Control and Prevention, seem to offer the best approach to reduce youth violence and produce long-term, lasting, positive results. These recommended strategies include: (1) Build strong families and communities and employ responsible parents as the chief agents to reduce youth violence; (2) Teach young children ways to resolve conflict peacefully; (3) Provide mentors to serve as guides and role models for positive youth behavior; (4) Reduce social and economic causes of violence in young people's environments; and (5) Ensure spiritual or character-based training for young children and reinforce that training throughout their early teen years. Where is the official U.S. government's response to 67,000 Black American citizens slaughtered in its streets during the past 9-1/2 years? Implementing solutions that effectively address this reign of death in the Black community will not and should not come primarily from Washington, state capitals or city halls. While it is the Black community that must strongly respond with effective solutions and actions, government still has a crucial responsibility to support structural remedies to this genocide. So far, local, state and federal governments alike have answered with a "calculated non-response" to the national carnage and human catastrophe of this Black-on- Black murder.

This same calculated non-response was the position taken by all levels of government during the reign of terror by the Ku Klux Klan. More than 145 years after the Klan's founding, only the killers have changed—not the killing, not the victims and not the poor response from government! Are young Black men doing the work of the Ku Klux Klan? They are doing it better than the Klan! And the world is watching. It is noted that although the reasoning for Black-on-Black killings may differ from the Klan's impetus, the results are in some black leaders words "arguably more horrific." The dates, parallel time lines, and related numbers sadly but factually speak for themselves. Noting a Tuskegee Institute study, a newsletter revealed that the Ku Klux Klan killed 3,446 Black people in America "during an 86-year span" as compared with Black men who kill about the same number of Black people "every six months."Backing up a Tuskegee documentation with this findings, authors Molefi K. Asante and Mark T. Mattson in their work "Historical and Cultural Atlas of African Americans" list that between the 29 years of 1889 and 1918 in the then 48 states from Alabama to Wyoming, 2,932 Black people were Comparatively, with our current 2010 Black-on-Black homicide stats, the authors chronicle the decade between 1890 and 1900 "as the most dangerous time" in the post Civil War era for Black men to be alive. They add that nearly 1,700 persons were lynched in that decade compared to 921 in the decade between 1900 and 1910; 840 from 1910 to 1920, and nearly 400 between 1920 and 1930. Again, comparatively speaking, that would be3,861 Black people killed by white hands between the 40 years of 1890 and 1930; still on the low end when measured against current day reported Black killings by Black hands. Statistics from the United States Department of Justice demonstrates the shockingly overwhelmed magnitude of this Black-on-Black reality during the nine-and-a-half year period from 2001 through 2010. In two U.S. wars, 6,754 American soldiers were killed including 2,019 soldiers in Afghanistan since 2001 and 4,735 soldiers in Iraq since 2003. Shockingly for our nation's central city communities, the newsletter released data would reveal that during this same nine-and-a-half years that the U.S. has been at war oversees from 2001 through 2010, approximately 67,000 Black people were murdered during this same time in the United States.

Yet another observer of stats comparing the killings of the Ku Klux Klan and the still growing Black- on-Black homicidal numbers is Clinton L. Black in his 2007 work "Why All Black People Are Coming to an End." According to his figures, the Ku Klux Klan lynched 3,437 Black men, women and children in the 115 years from 1866 to 1981. He writes, black people are murdering 3,437 Black men, women, and children in a 115 day period. Noting his findings, mathematically he postures that a Black person commits a crime against another Black person somewhere in America every second. His figures conclude that at this rate, that would be "six Black-on-black crimes a minute, 3,600 Black-on-Black crimes an hour, 86,400 Black-on-Black crimes a day, 604,800 Black-on-Black crimes a week, 2,629,743.83 Black-on-Black crimes a month The author contends that although the overwhelming majority of these crimes go unreported, this is still the most "devastating force" against Black people in the world today. Let's look at the numbers. For the purpose of this writing, we will use and anchor Black Star's figure of 67,000 Black-on-Black killings. Reviewing Black Star's Tuskegee figure of 3,447 Blacks killed by lynching, Black hands murdered 63,554 more Black folk then did whites during this present day period. Taking a look at Asante and Mattson's research of killings where 2,932 Blacks were lynched by whites. Black hands today murdered 64,068 more Black folk then did whites during the 29 years between 1889 and 1918. Since the U.S. has been at war oversees where approximately 6,754 American soldiers were killed, Black hands murdered 60,246 more Black folk then the numbers of reported Americans who died in Afghanistan and Iraq citing Black Star figures over the past nine-and-a-half- years from 2001 through 2010. And finally, we do not want to exclude author Clinton L. Black's findings. These are earlier times just think of how these numbers stand today. According to his figures, the Ku Klux Klan murdered 3, 437 Black men, women and children. Black hands killed 63,563 more Black people within the past 10 years than did the Klan over the 115 years from 1866 to 1981. But after her 1892 writing revealed names that were responsible for the lynching of three Memphis African Americans, a mob of whites demolished her printing press and office. They threatened to lynch Wells in front of the Memphis courthouse.

But there was nothing new about such threats on her life. She had received her share of threats and hostilities from white men. She fled to New York City where she was hired by an African American weekly and launched her anti-lynching campaign. The Black Star newsletter contends that there was a time when Black communities "wanted Black men to protect them from white men who wore 'hoods' while these whites killed Black people and destroyed their property." Now today, Black communities in this age of "A Black President" are no longer asking Black men to protect their families, women, children and property, but are pleading with (mostly white) police departments, state National Guard units and even the government to protect them/or us from our own Black males wearing "hoodies" and occasionally ski masks who are now in larger numbers killing Black people and destroying our property. "It's a Cultural Tragedy; no other people on earth hate, rape, rob, assault, envy, betray, distrust, kill, exterminate and outright violate Black people more than Black people! No other race of people in the whole world deliberately destroys their own people quite like Black people! In a real sense, we as a Black Community are a weapon of mass self- destruction!" says The Nation of Islam Leader Minister Louis Farrakhan. A 1982 study by sociologist Robert Staples titled, "Black Masculinity – The Black Male's Role in American Society," stated 28 to 30 years ago that: "The largest group responsible for homicides in this country is that of Black males in the 20 to 24-year age range. And their victims are similarly young Black men – a fact which has as its most tragic consequence that homicide is listed as the number one cause of death among Black males aged 15 to 30." We have top the Black-on-Black homicide rates of 67,000 Black people between 2001 through 2010 or the stat reflecting that as of 2007/08, Black males in the U.S. having been the lowest graduation rates amongst Black males as well as the College level. "Black students nationally are at rock bottom on SAT and ACT with no outcry or action from so call leaders.

These scores "predict" low college admission rates, high unemployment rates and high incarceration rates. Black students are in trouble!" As well as the Black Community is in trouble and a positive and prideful Black future is in serious danger. What is more concern is why is it that for decade, we are continually witnessing the black community and particularly our children dying as a result of a slow but readily visible, understandable and predictable self- imposed genocidal decay in our social, educational, political, and economic infrastructure while many of our so called black leaders, our ministers, our educators, our politicians, and our community stakeholders are saying and doing absolutely nothing. 145 years following 1865's Emancipation Proclamation, we can no longer use as an excuse or blame racism or White Supremacy for our Black community ills WE CANNOT!! Former President Barak Obama with the submission of any funds could not all of a sudden raise us up with proposals for solutions at which point all with a 501 © 3 response as though your organization all of a sudden has some unique insight as to why our young men are killing one another or why our Black males are not graduating or why our students are scoring low on the ACT or SAT. When he launched a massive pardon to all drug offenders who were wrongly and unjustified in here sentencing process to which many black males have been. It is us, our own people that have allowed this condition and self-destructive behavior to befall upon our youth as a result of our irresponsive inaction in these regard. Welcome to America where too many young Black men live short, desperate, miserable, complicated and violent lives. Recently a young Black man reported to the California General Assembly that the biggest challenge in his life was getting to school safely–not getting good grades or graduating from school, not wearing new clothes or even having a job, but just getting to school unscathed! Simply staying alive for 21 years is the number-one concern for many young Black men whose actions and inactions are influenced by their dire sense of hopelessness.

Seemingly random negative obstacles facing Black males in America constitute nothing less than a well- crafted, highly orchestrated system of mass destruction for young Black men and boys. Black men and boys are at the bottom of the educational system and the top of the criminal justice system. Their life expectancy and health indicators are the lowest in America and they top the homicide and violent-injury statistics throughout the nation. Black males also rank at the bottom in high-school and college-graduation rates and at the top of the official and unofficial unemployment rates. All social indicators in America predict a short, miserable life for those unlucky enough to be born Black males in America. To what extent do Americans know and care enough to stop this systematic genocide? The New Jim Crow, book had become an instant classic and staple for college undergraduate and graduate classes in law, political science, sociology and history nationwide. It peels back the layers of modern, systematic racism that have led to more Black men in America being imprisoned in 2011 than there were Black people enslaved in America in 1850. A new "caste" system of racial control also has more Black men imprisoned in the United States today than the combined number of people imprisoned in every other country worldwide. On top of all that, and reinforcing it, is an endlessly spouting sewer of racism in the media, culture and politics of this society—racism that takes deadly aim at the dreams and spirit of every Black American child. And who can forget the wave of nooses that sprung up around the country, south *and* north, in the wake of the 2007 struggle in Jena, Louisiana against the prosecution of six Black youth who had fought back against a noose being hung to intimidate them from sitting under a "whites only" tree at school? All this lay beneath the criminal government response to Hurricane Katrina in 2005. For reasons directly related to the oppression of Black people throughout the history of this country, and continuing today, Black Americas were disproportionately the ones without the resources to get out of the way of that storm, as well as the ones concentrated in the neighborhoods whose levees had gone unrepaired for years. Far from "mere" incompetence, the government responded with a combination of gun-in-your-face repression and wanton, murderous neglect. People were stuck on rooftops in 100-degree heat for days on end, with nothing to eat or drink. Prisoners were left locked in cells as waters rose to their necks. The protection of private property and social control was placed above human life.

The governor of the state ordered cops and soldiers to shoot on sight "looters"—that is, people trying to survive and to help others. On at least one occasion, people trying to escape the worst-hit areas were stopped by police at gunpoint from crossing over to a safer area.

When evacuations finally *were* carried out, they were done with the heartlessness of a cruel plantation owner. Families were separated, with children ripped away from parents. Tens of thousands were scattered all over the country with one-way tickets, sometimes not even told their destinations. Back home, bodies were left floating in water, or lying on sidewalks, underneath debris, decomposing and mangled for months. Through it all, politicians and commentators spewed out unrelenting racism. " A 10-term Congressman took the prize for declaring, "We finally cleaned up public housing in New Orleans. We couldn't do it, but God did." But where are we all today entering into 2025. What will life be like in the year 2025 and beyond. " FIND YOURSELF "

CHAPTER VI

HONOR AND FREEDOM

Japanese culture is structured around black and white norms for acceptable (harmony-producing) group behavior. People who don't function by these norms are viewed as outsiders who lack legitimate status. Black and white expectations of behavior produce equally clear cut conformity, resulting in high harmony and certainty of outcome. Trust is earned through continuous conformity. This is a match for elements of Biblical behavior we have noted: the placement of group expectations over individual behavior. It also is similar to a concept we have noted of "black and white" attitudes in such passages as Luke 14:26., an Extremity of language and extremity of action 2). Harmony is the number one priority in Japanese interpersonal and social behavior taking priority over frankness and honesty. The same may be said in the Biblical world. The demands of honor mean that harmony of this sort is a priority, even to the point of sometimes committing an "honorable lie" to preserve order. 3). Behavioral skills in the workplace are more important to success than analytical skills. Correct etiquette (processes) is more important than personal performance. The Japanese react far more than they proact, like pinballs bouncing off the bumpers. Adaptation is of supreme importance to success. Etiquette is the principle of behavior rather than philosophy or religion. Accountability is to the group, not the individual. The big picture is the only picture. Conformity produces harmony, the supreme value. It is noted with the Hebraic notion of knowledge as entailing action, and accountability to a group for church discipline. "The big picture is the Biblical emphasis on the corporate body of Christ."Conformity produces harmony"; with the admonishments to live peacefully with all. 4). The Japanese strive to meet the expectations of others, especially those in power. Doing something in the right (role model) way is more important than achieving a favorable outcome. A glorious defeat is better than victory achieved with the wrong (nonconforming) attitude. Behavioral models save the Japanese worker from embarrassment. Unstructured social situations are therefore to be avoided at all costs. Trust is essential in Japanese relationships, but the trust is based on predictability of behavior rather than emotional rapport or intimate friendship. If all the Japanese in Japan were lined up and asked to describe Americans and other Westerners in one word, the majority would probably come up with "selfish." The reason for this is simple enough.

The Japanese were conditioned for centuries to look upon independent, individualistic behavior the hallmark of Americans and many other Westerners as selfish, confrontational and disruptive. Outsiders are perceived as barbarians because they don't conform to cultural mandates and because no loyalty is owed to them. Independence is a social stigma; interdependence brings identity, acceptance, security, and a sense of purpose. All behaviors must focus on concern for the other person's mental harmony and face (wah). Behaviors lacking wah are relationship damaging: Criticizing in public; blame-placing; singling out others for praise; dominating conversations or interrupting others; pointing out mistakes or errors. Employee motivation is a balance of internal and external forces, coming from strong role expectations and the strong desire to maintain personal identity through meeting these expectations. Cultural behavior is based on mutual interdependencies that create both power and weakness. This is a key source of stress in Japanese society, because there is no closure of interpersonal and social obligations. Independence is never attained. The Japanese kaisha ("guy-shah") is held together by networks of hierarchical relationships from which individual employees receive their identity and status. To lose ones standing and legitimacy in the kaisha is to lose one's identity. Permanent employment is therefore the expectation and tradition. Japan's news media often report that well over half of all Japanese are so seriously afflicted by stress that it is a problem of epidemic proportions. Part of this affliction results from the intense pressure on people to work harder and produce more than other people. Stress also results from crowded living conditions and from worry about financial security during old age. Much of the stress experienced by the Japanese derives from conforming to the demands of their traditional social system—part of which is a tendency to be compulsive about things. A big difference lies in the economic reality. In the ancient world you were never "unemployed" because you a ways found it necessary to look for sustenance. Worry about old age and security could be had, but the ancients were less able to do something about it. Note nevertheless in this respect Jesus' admonition not to worry about such things. Traditional Japanese have tried to maintain and balance two worlds. One consisted of reality or hone (hone-nay)—their true thoughts and intentions—and the other of a facade or tatemae ("tah-tay-my)—a screen created to maintain the appearance of harmony and serve as a ploy until the other party revealed their own position.

The Japanese reaction to new relations was that they could not be established because no relations existed. There had to be some kind of recognized outside connection bringing the two parties together—a go-between or some other third party. Most traditional Japanese go to great lengths to avoid confrontations with others. They are quick to apologize and accept personal responsibility in case something might be wrong or possibly go wrong.   Superiors may often accept personal blame for the failures of subordinates in a project or for their breach of etiquette or failure to live up to expectations. There is a perfectly good word for "no" in the Japanese language, but it is seldom used. "Yes," on the other hand, is heard all the time. This does not mean, however, that the Japanese do not say "no." They say it often, even if what they have said sounds like "yes" to the uninitiated. For many generations the Japanese were conditioned to avoid blunt responses, confrontations or friction of any kind. Since "no" is often confrontational and can cause disappointment and ill will of one kind or another, the Japanese do not like to come right out and say it. As a result, "yes" gradually came to by synonymous with "Yes, I heard you," or "Yes, I am listening." It ceased to mean "Yes, I agree" or "Yes, I will." The main   reason for this development was the overriding need to maintain harmony, and the importance of self-preservation. Many Westerners, particularly Americans, have been conditioned to view time as something like a train speeding down a straight track.   The train never slows down or stops and they have a compulsive, deep-seated need to be on it, moving toward specific goals. Japanese, on the other hand, have traditionally viewed the time track as a circle, with the train moving slowly and repeatedly passing the same place over a period of time. One of the most common and important time factors in Japanese negotiations or discussions about serious matters was—and still is—the use of time gaps or breaks. The people involved simply stop talking. They may just sit and remain silent (often with their eyes closed), get up and leave the room for short periods, or hold low-voiced side conversations with their colleagues. Japanese negotiators and others develop varying degrees of skill in using these time gaps to their own advantage. Ato Aji ("Ah-toe Ah-jee") Leaving an aftertaste: Foreign things have a different "taste" that Japanese may or may not find palatable.   Among those things that are acceptable are apparel, accessories, foods and other consumer tangibles, as well as movies, athletic studios, and music.

Those that will leave an undesirable ato aji or "aftertaste" include people from any other race or ethnic group, and their unstructured, unpredictable behavior. The country is no longer in a position to close its borders, leaving the Japanese with no choice but to develop a tolerance and appreciation for other people who "taste" different. This overview of Japanese history from the earliest times to the present unlike China and Korea, the borders of Japan have stayed relatively stable throughout most of its history due to its geographic status as a group of islands. Until the mid-20th century, historic Japan was never occupied by another people and in turn never held territorial possessions on the mainland or major islands nearby until the late 19th century– though attempts were made at colonizing the Korean peninsula in the late 16th century. From the late 19th century until 1945, the imperial Japanese government had colonies in Taiwan, Korea, and northeast China and, during WWII, major parts of Southeast Asia. Since 1945, Japan has remained in its traditional territory, though a few islands are still held in dispute with various states in the region. The Japanese people of today seem to have had ancestors that came from several places. Although in antiquity the mountainous islands were once connected to the mainland, after the last Ice Age, the waters rose, isolating the island group. Whatever the origins of the earliest inhabitants were, some groups may have come from nearby Siberia, the Korean peninsula, the Yellow River and Yangzi River areas of present-day China and the southern chain of islands that lead down into Polynesia. By at least 300 BC, significant populations with advanced metal technology, rice agriculture, and horses began arriving from the Korean peninsula, and the dates of such migrations may yet be pushed back farther. As culture developed in Japan, there were several periods when archaeological and historical evidence point to the rapid introduction of cultural elements from other places. These cultural borrowings were subsequently re-made in Japan to fit local needs and tastes. In some periods, cultural borrowing proceeded in a systematic matter, with definite goals in mind. This process of controlled selection and adaptation was enhanced by the island nature of the country. The Age of Reform (552-710 AD), the Meiji Period (1868-1912), and the decades right after WWII are three prominent examples. In studying modern Japanese culture, it is still possible to see layers of these influences from the past.

At various times in history, the major sources of these influences have been states on the Korean peninsula, Silk Road cultures, China, Europe, and the United States. After periods of intense borrowing, Japan has often withdrawn into itself and the foreign cultural influences have become Japanese, sometimes taking new and creative directions. A good example would be certain styles of Japanese art and architecture that were once based on Chinese models. It is interesting to note that in some instances the successes at borrowing and remaking were wildly successful—the modern auto industry, for example. Other experiments in cultural borrowings sometimes took unexpected directions. A good example is the attempt to introduce the Chinese-style of imperial government starting in the 7th century AD. Although certain codes and reforms were established for several centuries, the grand experiment was largely abandoned by the late 12th century, when a form of Japanese feudalism arose. In this new system, the emperor became a divine figurehead, while real power lay in the hands of the paramount military leader known as the shogun. This era gave way to a culture of warrior-aesthetes, quite distinct from the clearer separation between civil and military cultures in the Chinese state. Today, Japan is a super-modern and developed country that is still able to hold onto selected vestiges of its rich cultural heritage. Tokyo and Osaka are highly cosmopolitan cities that feature cultural elements from all over the globe. Yet, a Japanes aesthetic prevails as past and present cultural influences continue to interweave in one of the most powerful engines of popular culture on earth. The evidence of chipped stone tools suggests that humans inhabited Japan at least 30,000 years ago. "Neolithic" cultures called "Jomon" (that still retained stone tool traits of earlier periods), date to at least 10,000 BC. The Jomon people were hunters and gatherers who lived upon the rich resources of game, fish, and wild plants native to post-Ice Age Japan. One of the unusual features of Jomon culture is pottery—the oldest reliably dated on earth. By 8,000 BC a type of cord-wrapped pottery—with decorated lines made by wrapping or laying cords on wet clay developed. Other clay objects are the so-called dogu ("earth god") figurines. These are small statues that look something like "extra-terrestrials" (or Pokemon cartoon figures!) that may have been used in fertility worship. Always few in number, the Jomon peoples seem to have been centered on the Kanto plain area of Honshu Island. Japan first appears in the historical records of China in about 300 BC.

In those records the inhabitants of Japan were known as the Wa. The records tell of a Queen named Pimiko (Himiko) who had a tribal domain in the southwest areas of Honshu and Kyushu. According to the accounts she lived in a hill-top fortress and was waited upon by 1,000 young women. Her brother handled communications outside the walls, acting as a sort of regent. The queen may have had a dual role as a type of shaman with links to the spirit world. It is not known if she was related to the gods. Eventually, Japanese emperors would trace descent directly to the Sun Goddess, Amaterasu, who along with her brother, were instrumental in the creation story of Japan. During the Yayoi period a number of new technological and agricultural elements arrived from the Asian mainland, most probably by boat from the Korean peninsula. Among the new cultural attributes were wet-rice agriculture, bronze and iron, new styles of pottery, livestock, and a whole host of cultural patterns having to do with village and elite life. Most likely, these elements of culture were carried to Japan by waves of immigrants who settled around the land, gradually displacing or absorbing the native populations. It is unclear how the aboriginal Ainu fit into the picture of these early periods of Japan, but warfare with displaced tribes continued for centuries. By the Tomb Period population centers had grown up in several parts of the islands and the roots of city culture had taken place. Contact with cultures in China and especially the Korean peninsula continued. With the exception of the northern wilderness of Hokkaido and parts of southern Kyushu, clans known as uji controlled many portions of the islands. Chinese records from the latter part of the era tell of a powerful uji family known as the Yamato, located in the plain between the present cities of Nara and Osaka. By this time a stratified society had developed consisting of rulers, craftsmen, farmers, and even some slaves. The Yamato were only one of many tribal units, which according to Chinese records, fought incessantly among each other. The Yamato had relations with China, as well as several states on the Korean peninsula. The present emperor of Japan traces his descent to the Yamato ruling family. The Yamato Plain region is the site of the oldest tomb mounds in Japan. These tomb mounds (kofun) are in some ways similar to earlier ones found in China and those on the Korean peninsula from around the same time frame. A number of huge mounds are in the shape of an old-fashioned key-hole, though many smaller ones were hemispherical in shape.

A style of clay sculpture known as haniwa is associated with some of the grave mounds. The haniwa are earthenware pottery made of hollow tubes of clay. The subjects are abstracted humans of various occupations, farm animals, houses, boats, and other items. In ways they are similar in spirit to the clay items placed in graves in Han dynasty China. In some cases the inside of the larger tombs were decorated with murals, as seen in early China and Korea. By the fifth century, models of horses and bronze horse tack appear, along with more sophisticated metal swords, bows and arrow, and spears. Influences from China and other mainland civilizations on the Silk Road made their way into Japan via people moving to and from on the waters of the Tsushima Straits between Japan and Korea and the greater Yellow Sea interaction sphere. By 607 AD a ruler in Japan by the name of Prince Shotoku (574-622) sent a mission of monks, government representatives, and students on a prolonged study abroad program to China in order to increase the rate of importation of the positive aspects of Chinese culture. Among the imports were literacy in Chinese (Shotoku had a Korean scribe to help with this task), Buddhism, art, customs, and principles of Chinese rule. The gifted prince, regent for his mother, the Empress Suiko, commissioned a temple complex at present day Horyuji. He also drafted Japans first written government constitution, namely the 17 Article Constitutions. As time went on, over six missions were sent to China, and reforms were instituted in Japan, first in the Yamato court, then elsewhere. In 645 AD, a reformer named Fujiwara no Kamatari (614-669) extended the implementation of the Chinese model of government by canonizing a set of legal reforms known as the Taika Reforms. Later, the Emperor Temmu (reigned 672-686) introduced more institutional and legal reforms on the model of Tang dynasty, China. In a break with the past (and in imitation of the Chinese "son of heaven"), he took the title of "heavenly emperor (tenno), rather than king. In 702 AD, another set of legal guidelines called the Taiho Code were drawn up in an attempt to resolve contradictions between government interests in taxation and the landholdings of large uji, who were in constant factional struggles over power with the centralized government. Eventually monasteries and large estates gained a special tax-exempt status, and the peasants shouldered the burden of taxation. During the Age of Reform, the Japanese set in place the foundations for an experiment in Chinese-style rule that would bear fruit in an elite culture unrivaled in Japanese history, lasting until the late 12th century.

The next two eras, the Nara and Heian, are known as the classical age of Japan. Nara is regarded as the first permanent capital in Japan. Before that time the capital was relocated at the demise of each ruler due to taboos involving pollution of the living site by death. Following the Chinese model of a permanent seat of government, the new capital was modeled on the capital of Tang China, Chang an (today's Xi'an city). The earliest part of the city (which was on a much smaller scale than Chang and without a wall) was based on a rectangle of eight squares, built on a north to south axis with streets running through them in a neat grid pattern. The city was divided into two halves: the Left Capital and the Right Capital. The new palace was placed to the north. A major causeway, called the Scarlet Phoenix Avenue, ran down the middle of the city, leading to the palace After its establishment in 710 AD, Nara would become a city renowned even today for its architecture and tradition of Buddhist art. Although the structures remaining in Nara today were built in later centuries, many were constructed on sites dating to the earliest years of the kingdom. Some of the best descriptions of these early sites come from a huge tourist guidebook compiled by a poet and printed in 1681. Much of what is known about life in the Nara period centers on the lifestyles of the elite in the capital cities. The use of Chinese as a literary language increased throughout the Nara period. An example of the sustained influence of Chinese culture on the elite was the first collection of Japanese poems, known as the Ten Thousand Leaves, or Manyoshu. Buddhism became an important force in the capital and was patronized by the government. Statues of Buddha were commissioned, 48 temples built within Nara and many more throughout the land, and Buddhist scriptures were mass-produced and spread everywhere. A scandal late in the period involved a powerful Buddhist monk who manipulated the ruling empress and nearly took control of the throne. Although a number of women had ruled in Japan (usually after the death of their husbands), this custom was brought to an end because of the scandal. Although the capital city and other upper-class echelons were developed under the influence of imported Chinese culture, the rural villages and farmsteads were much more conservative. Farmers in some areas lived in pit houses partially underground and farmed wet-rice.

Dry land fields were still cleared by swidden agricultural techniques that involved burning off brushy and forested areas and planting in the ash-rich soil. The Nara period was characterized by continued importation of Chinese culture and the spread of Buddhism. In the next period, the Heian period, the Chinese influences would be re-made with Japanese characteristics, in some cases preserving aspects of Chinese culture that were long out of fashion in China. In 794 AD a new capital was founded at Heian, the site of the present city of Kyoto. The Heian period would prove to be the height of classical culture in ancient Japan. The samurai of later ages would look back to Heian as a source of patterns of elite culture, which they wove into their more militaristic outlook. Again taking the Tang dynasty capital as a model, the new city was a third the size of Chang'an (Xi'an) and had a low wall. Heian is the age of the Shining Prince"—the age of Prince Genji, the major character in the Lady Murasaki Shibuku's Tale of Genji. Based on accounts of Japanese and Western visitors, Ivan Morris gives a description of the setting of the capital in the pre-industrialized era: The capital itself was situated in beautiful country, encircled on three sides by thickly forested hills and mountains, often delicately wreathed with trails of mist; in the autumn evenings one could hear the deer's cry in the distance and the desolate call of the wild geese overhead; the landscape abounded in streams and waterfalls and lakes; and into its green slopes and valleys the countless shrines and monasteries blended as if they too had become a part of nature. Life at the courts became insulated from the rest of the world and the relative peace of most of the era allowed for a flowering of culture. New forms of writing called kana were created that easily reflected the sounds of the Japanese language. Although much easier than learning classical Chinese, scholars and bureaucrats preferred Chinese and its elite associations, while the new written language was soon used by court women as a new medium for writing prose. Court women such as Sei Shonagon and Murasaki Shikibu contributed to the creation of a women literature that rivaled any prose writings in the world of that time—though of course it was entirely unknown outside of a tiny audience in Japan. One of the aesthetic principles reflected in the literature of the period was that of miyabi, or courtly elegance. The term appears hundreds of times in the Tale of Genji and refers to the gentle, often ritualized, and sensitive manners cultivated by the elite of the time.

Another important aesthetic element that evolved further with introduction of Zen Buddhism in later centuries is the concept of mono no aware, or sensitivity to things. Enhanced by the natural beauty of Japan, the aesthetic was based on the idea that the heart/soul is stimulated by images of the sublime in nature. Thus, a falling cherry blossom or an autumn leaf circling in a pool creates subtle and indescribable feelings that can only be expressed by poetry or other arts. A related concept is that of wabi, the effect of construed naturalness exhibited in an artwork such as the cracks or irregularities in the glaze on a tea bowl that reflect the effects of primitive firing techniques. These aesthetics are also part of the appreciation of Japanese garden architecture. Cultivation of the aesthetics, linked with meditation, became an important dimension of the warrior samurai culture in later eras of Japanese history. Courtly refinement and aesthetic sensitivity were reflected in the daily dress and manners of the elite. Both men and women's clothing and adornment were subject to conventions of the day. Women wore an elaborate costume of up to twelve inner and outer layers of cloth. Natural white teeth were colored black with a solution of iron and powdered gallnut soaked in vinegar (temporary teeth blackening remains as a part of the process of becoming a geisha entertainer in Kyoto today). Hair was decorated with ornaments and worn as long as possible even to the ground. White powder was applied to the face and neck and light rouge on the cheeks. Eyebrows were plucked and misty dark blotches were painted high upon the forehead. Lips were painted red like tiny flower buds. Like the standards for Tang dynasty women, Heian women cultivated full figures (although bodies were not displayed in public, hidden beneath the mounds of cloth). Elite women were educated in calligraphy, poetry, music, and customs such as incense preparation, which allowed them some intellectual parity with men of their class with similar training. Although most upper class women spent their days in secluded leisure at home, possibly engaging in embroidery and dyeing cloth, women of the court like Sei Shonagon, had somewhat more public lives. Interactions between the sexes (other than close family members and lovers) were rarely direct. Communication, when necessary, was often through carefully crafted letters delivered by go-betweens or servants. Elite men led much more public lives, involved in politics and the running of their estates.

Although the power of Buddhism was not allowed to increase to the point it had in Nara, a new form of Buddhism that offered salvation to all believers was imported from China by a monk named Saicho (767-822 AD). The new Tendai (Tiantai) beliefs soon became widespread among the nobles and the populace. Many great temples and monasteries of several sects of Buddhism remain in Kyoto today, as living testaments of the great Buddhist tradition in Japan. During the Heian period, the experiments with centralized Chinese rule and taxation gradually faded into a situation with a weak central government ruled by an emperor that was increasingly a figurehead. Large clan families like the Fujiwara, Minamoto, and Taira increased their power and holdings and came into conflict with each other and other families over control of the realm. The turmoil of the Kamakura period contrasts sharply with the refined atmosphere associated with the classic age of Heian culture. During this period, attempts were made at ruling Japan through a centralized Imperial Chinese model, backed by civil codes, which evolved into a system similar in spirit and substance to feudalism in Europe. In this epoch, the warrior class of samurai takes the stage, and militancy becomes the social and political norm. The role of the emperor becomes almost wholly ceremonial, as the military side of the government, under the leadership of the shogun (generalissimo of the Imperial Army), took actual control of policy and implementation. By the end of the era, Japan would become an island nation filled with warring armies associated with rival family domains struggling for political and military dominance. Yoritomo Minamoto the era began with the rise of the first shogun. As the winner in a prolonged struggle between the Fujiwara, Taira, and Minamoto families for control of the realm, a general named Yoritomo Minamoto (1147-1199 AD) set up a new government in the Kanto plain, quite close to the present city of Tokyo. At this moment, real power shifted from the western Kansai region around Heian (Kyoto) to Yoritomos military government at Kamakura. The new government was called bakufu or tent government, suggesting a military encampment. Although the emperor continued to exist in Kyoto, and was acknowledged by Yoritomo and succeeding shoguns, from this point on (with one brief exception), the role of the emperor would be minimal until the Meiji Restoration in 1867. Yoritomo simplified the government processes and instituted a basic legal code, although the court in Kyoto retained much of its form and administrative function.

Large family domains retained varying numbers of samurai professional military men something like the knights of Europe. Common people tilled the land, much as they had always done. The era began with the rise of the first shogun as the winner in a prolonged struggle between the Fujiwara, Taira, and Minamoto families for control of the realm, a general named Yoritomo Minamoto (1147-1199AD) set up a new government in the Kanto plain, quite close to the present city of Tokyo. At this moment, real power shifted from the western Kansai region around Heian (Kyoto) to Yoritomos military government at Kamakura. The new government was called bakufu or tent government, suggesting a military encampment. Although the emperor continued to exist in Kyoto, and was acknowledged by Yoritomo and succeeding shoguns, from this point on (with one brief exception), the role of the emperor would be minimal until the Meiji Restoration in 1867. Yoritomo simplified the government processes and instituted a basic legal code, although the court in Kyoto retained much of its form and administrative function. Large family domains retained varying numbers of samurai professional military men something like the knights of Europe. Common people tilled the land, much as they had always done. The greatest threat to Japanese sovereignty before the great changes of the 19th and 20th centuries came during the Kamakura period with the attempts by the Mongols of Kublai Khan to invade Japan. Two major attempts, seven years apart in the late 13th century were launched from the Korean peninsula. The Mongols commandeered thousands of ships, boats and crews from Korea and China in the invasions. The samurai warriors who still used one on one battle tactics based on horseback archery, then swords (once on the ground), put up a stiff resistance against the Mongol forces, but ultimately would have been little match for the coordinated military tactics of massed archers, fire bombs, and siege weapons in the Mongol military arsenal. The Mongols, however, seem to have been no match for the protective kami (local gods) of Japan, who sent ravaging typhoons (the "divine winds or kamikaze) that twice sunk the Mongol fleets before full-scale invasions could take place. Nevertheless, the lingering fear of Mongol attacks only strengthened military culture in Japan, which continued to develop in the ensuing centuries of unrest. A very short period in Japanese history marked the transition between the Kamakura and Muromachi Period. This era is known as the Kemmu Restoration and is the last time a Japanese emperor attempted by force to take control of Japan.

This occurred in 1333, when Emperor Go-Daigo attempted to re-institute direct imperial rule by amassing forces against the bakufu government of the prevailing shogun. Emperor Go-Daigo sent his troops under the leadership of General Ashikaga Takauji to route the resisting factions. In the course of events Go-Daigo gave support to some of Ashikagas rivals, which in turn stimulated Ashikaga to turn the tables. Returning to Kyoto, he drove Go-Daigo into the hills, and managed to place a new emperor (from another imperial line) on the throne. Nevertheless, Go-Daigo set up a government in exile in southern Japan that lasted for several decades. This event ushered in an era of almost constant marital strife between the regional domains in Japan, as local lords contested for the position of shogun and the hierarchical feudal system further developed. Although fate intervened to save Japan from the Mongols, the Mongol invasions brought instability to the emerging Japanese feudal system, which eventually descended into a state of turmoil and incessant fighting between local warlords. No one leader managed to gain firm control over the entire realm at this time. Though Kyoto continued as a grand capital, the base of military power was in Kamakura. During this period feudalism developed further. The emperor (dwelling in Kyoto) was the divine leader of the land, though functioned more as a figurehead who gave legitimacy to the rule of the shogun. The shogun, who usually resided in the court at Kamakura (near modern-day Tokyo), held the reigns of true power over the regional lords. The regional lords all employed armies of samurai, and below them were the townspeople and peasant farmers. The samurai code of service demanded loyalty to lord and one's family name as well as self-discipline and perfection in the martial arts. Dishonor was the occasion for ritual suicide by sword. During this period a new literature emerged, often on martial themes. The aesthetic of such works is that of sabi, which reflected a deep melancholy or sadness over the brevity of existence. The Tale of Heike is the best-known of these martial works. In this era a samurai might contemplate the beauty of a meadow flower in one instant, and engage in mortal combat in another (as exemplified in a famous scene in the Akira Kurosawa film, Seven Samurai). More popular forms of Buddhism like the Pure Land (Jodo) and Nichiren sects were spread throughout the populace.

Zen Buddhism, which arrived from the mainland in 1191 via a monk named Eisai (who also introduced the tea ritual), became of great interest to the samurai warrior class in part because of its stress on the exacting discipline of the meditation process. The Onin Wars (1467-77 AD) was the most bloody and chaotic moment of the period, and destruction was widespread. Kyoto was largely destroyed in the feuds between two great families that spilled into other parts of the realm. The devastating war signaled the beginning of over a hundred years of chaos and strife. Due to a breakdown in what central control there was, social mobility increased between classes and regional overlords competed for soldiers and labor to further their interests. Armies of foot soldiers amassed from the peasantry were now used in warfare. At first armed with spears and pikes, by the end of the era massed contingents of foot soldiers with firearms were used decisively in battle. Oda Nobunaga, the latter period of the era (1568-1600 AD) is known as the Age of Reunification. During this period the number of local lords lessened, though those remaining in the struggles grew in power. These super-lords were known as daimyo. The three great daimyo in the final decades were Oda Nobunaga (1534-82 AD), the commoner Hideyoshi (1536-98 AD), and a somewhat younger leader in Oda Nobunaga's retinue named Tokugawa Ieyasu (1543-1616 AD).   All three men attempted to unify Japan by creating (or forcing) alliances among the powerful daimyo of the land. Oda Nobunaga was known as a fierce and relentless warrior whose armies were equipped with matchlock firearms introduced by shipwrecked Portugeuse sailors around 1543. Oda managed to extend his rule over a number of the contending daimyo until his assassination at the hands of a rival whom he light-heartedly struck on the head with a fan at a banquet. Known as the namban (southern barbarians), the Portuguese were later followed by the Spanish. The newcomers had similar goals: trade and conversion of souls to Christianity an attitude different from the Dutch and British who wanted only trade and plunder. Jesuit priests from Portugal and Spain soon brought Christianity to Japan where it had a mixed reception. Although at one point a following of an estimated two million was gained, unlike Buddhism, the new faith demanded the forsaking of all other beliefs and required allegiance to a foreign and far away leader in the Vatican. Some Japanese leaders like Oda Nobunaga attempted to use Christianity as a political force (in his case, against the rich Buddhist factions), while others like Tokugawa Ieyasu saw it as a destabilizing force.

The new religion was virtually eliminated from Japan in a series of intense purges around 1630 when thousands of leaders and followers were crucified. Some aspects of the contradictions between these competing foreign and native forces were included in the plot of the novel Shogun, and the film of the same name. Hideyoshi was a former peasant and vassal of Oda Nobunaga who managed to consolidate an even greater number of daimyo than his former lord. As part of his bid for control of Japan, he decreed that townspeople were to remain in towns and peasants were to remain in rural areas, thus lessening mobility between classes. Class divisions were starkly re-emphasized by a great sword hunt in which arms were collected from the common people and melted into Buddhist statues. The superior status of the samurai warriors (even lower level ones) was demonstrated by allowing them to continue wearing two swords in public (one long and one short). In an attempt to display his power, in the late 1500s Hideyoshi twice sent forces up the Korean peninsula in attempts to conquer the declining Ming dynasty in China that had been constantly pestered by attacks from Japanese pirates. The Japanese fleet was devastated by the armored turtle boats of Korean General Yi Soon-sin and huge numbers of Chinese soldiers that were sent across the northern borders of Choson Korea during the second attack. The mad plans to invade China ended (for the time being) with Hideyoshis sudden death in 1598. As the 16th century came to a close, a great battle between contending daimyo took place at Sekigahara in 1600 on the southwest coast. The forces of the patient and methodological Tokugawa Ieyasu won the day, and he soon unified the contending daimyo realms under a new form of centralized feudal state. Within a decade after the battle of Sekigahara, Tokugawa Ieyasu had established complete control over Japan. He established his shogunate in Edo, now modern Tokyo, though the emperor continued to reside in Kyoto. The innovations that the new shogun put in place would eventually create the conditions for Japans swift entrance into the modern world in the mid-19th century. In order to retain control over the realm, Tokugawa Ieyasu created a centralized bureaucracy, again inspired by the Chinese form of government, including ministries to oversee the administration of the state. He also instituted a number of policies to control the daimyo, who had been given lands close to the capital (the inner daimyo) or on the fringes (the outer daimyo) in accord to their allegiance (or lack of) during the late Ashikaga wars.

These policies included regular service to the realm, required upkeep of local castles and other assets, and visits to the capital every other year. This policy was enforced by requiring the local daimyo to lodge their immediate families in Edo. Thus there was a constant coming and going of great processions from the realms of the daimyo along the roadways linking parts of the islands. All this travel was good for the economy, however, and service and supply industries arose along the routes to the capital to feed, lodge, and provide necessities such as footwear, to the retinues. Another policy of control had to due with foreign relations. After the expulsion of foreigners (primarily Portuguese and Spanish) and the anti-Christian campaigns, the government followed a policy of seclusion. The fleets were allowed to fall into disuse (which coincidentally ended the problem of piracy that had plagued China and Korea) and trade was severely limited. No citizen, under threat of death, was allowed to freely leave Japan. The Dutch were eventually granted trading privileges at Decima Island near Nagasaki and the knowledge of European advances in science, medicine, and technology brought by them was known as Dutch learning." Honor And Freedom   Some trade was still carried on with the Chinese. Although not completely sealed off, for 250 years Japan remained for the most part in peaceful cloister from the rest of the world. Kabuki drama performance during the long period of peace in the Tokugawa period the position of the samurai gradually changed. Many filled the layers of central and local government. With no wars to fight, martial training became more ritualized and inter-mixed with revived aesthetics of the Heian period and Zen Buddhism. This is reflected in the samurai tastes for the austere Noh drama, the spartan tea ritual, flower arranging (ikebana), refined incense identification games (something like modern wine tasting), and haiku poetry. Economically, the samurai class (whose members were paid by the great landholders or government in rice) was in decline by the early 19th century. The merchant class, which had been slowly rising since the end of the Ashikaga period, became economically dominant as middle-classes composed of traders, shopkeepers, money-lenders, and transport agents arose in cities like Edo and Osaka. Enterprises combining production and distribution run by wealthy merchant families like Mitsui and Mitsubishi were precursors of modern multi-national companies. A strong money economy, (rooted in the Ashikaga period when coinage was actually imported from China), was supported by banking and lending institutions.

Huge entertainments districts featured boisterous kabuki theater, lively Bunraku puppet shows (with wooden puppets 2/3 life-size), and comic storytellers, as well as drinking and delights of the flesh. The milieu of this floating world of entertainment was reflected in thematic painting and woodblock prints of the age. Education was also of great importance and the literacy rate in urban Japan was high due in part to government sponsorship of schools and widespread printing technology (aided by earlier advances by Korea in the development of moveable metal type). Neo-Confucianism found a following and was promoted by the Tokugawa government that found its secular principles useful in establishing its centralized bureaucracy. Such were the dynamics in a society that would meet its destiny with the industrializing West with the arrival of American gunboats in the mid-19th century.   In 1853 Commodore Matthew C. Perry (grandson of Admiral Oliver Hazard Perry, the hero of the Battle of Lake Erie in 1812) sailed into Tokyo Bay with a small fleet of "black ships" and demanded that Japan open its ports to trade. Aware of the defeat of China at the hands of the British in the recent Opium War, Japan signed treaties with the United States of America in 1854, and a host of other countries including Great Britain, France, Holland, and Russia soon after. Clauses for "most-favored nation" status were demanded in these treaties, which allowed any privileges extended to any one of the foreign powers to be extended to them all. Townshend Harris (played by John Wayne in the 1960s film The Barbarian and the Geisha) the first American diplomat to live on Japanese soil gradually improved relations between the US and Japan. Nevertheless, as foreign legations were established throughout the land, humiliating incidents occurred, and a movement began to Revere the Emperor; expel the barbarian! Eventually an event involving the murder of a British merchant stimulated Britain to fire on a Japanese port. Seeing the power of British guns first-hand, the local daimyo befriended the British captain, and Japan was on its way to imitating the British navy. Ultimately, the Tokugawa shogunate was blamed for signing treaties with the foreigners and a movement among the nobles (many of them the descendants of the outer daimyo sent to the fringes by Tokugawa Ieyasu 250 years earlier) eventually swept the last shogun from power. In 1868, a young emperor, aged 16, was set on the throne and with a group of enlightened advisors set out to beat the foreigners at their own game. The new reign was called Meiji. From this time on, Japanese history would be divided into periods in accord with the reign of an individual emperor. Within a few years, Western-styled navy (copying Britain), army (copying Prussia), industry, banking, legal, and parliamentary systems were eventually introduced. The government also moved to set up railroads, textile mills, and other industries that were in some cases later turned over to the private sector. These changes were largely financed by increasing the tax burden on the peasants and merchants, rather than taking out huge foreign loans.

Though Neo-Confucianism was for a time influential in promoting the role of the emperor, Shinto was adopted as a state religion in that the emperor was literally seen as descending from the early kami. Saigo Takamori statue in Ueno Park In a backlash to these sudden changes, a group of samurai staged the so-called Satsuma Rebellion in 1877. This rebellion was an attempt to save the faltering status of the samurai class, which was being made irrelevant by the new conscript army armed with repeating firearms and modern cannon. The leader, the once-loyal adviser Saigo Takamori, committed suicide on the battlefield in a final fray between modern troops and mounted samurai warriors an event similar to that in the recent film, The Last Samurai. By 1895 Japan had defeated China in a series of land and sea battles around the Korean peninsula known as the Sino-Japanese War. The victory allowed Japan to gain a foothold in Korea and influence on the nearby Liaodong Peninsula of China. In 1905, the Japanese won a major war against imperial Russia on the Liaodong Peninsula, fought over a new railroad, timber, and seaports in Manchuria a very strategic corner of East Asia. Casualties were extremely high (over 20,000 in some battles) on both sides due to mechanized firearms and mass, suicidal charges by Japanese troops still motivated by samurai ethics that regarded surrender as dishonorable. Beginning with a surprise attack on the Russian navy, the deciding battle in the Tsushima straits between Korea and Japan resulted in a crippling Russian loss of 33 out of 35 ships sunk effectively neutering Russian naval influence in East Asia. In many ways this war was a harbinger for Japanese military actions up through the end of World War II and in part explains the calculation to attack Pearl Harbor.

As a result of their 1905 victory and the impending collapse of the Qing dynasty in China, Korea was colonized by the Japanese in 1910. Although a democratic, parliamentary society was being created in Japan in the early decades of the 20th century (universal male suffrage was established in 1925), the Great Depression in the early 1920s helped a radical wing of the Japanese military rise to power. Powerful government-supported companies called zaibatsu aided in creating an effective and modern war machine, unlike anything seen outside of Europe and the United States in World War I. By the mid-1920s, imperial Japan had extended itself further into Manchuria, and a full-scale invasion in China was underway by the mid-1930s. By the early 1940s the powerful Japanese navy, army, and air forces had enabled Japan to secure most of the former European colonies in East Asia, Southeast Asia, and the Pacific Islands. They were also positioned to threaten Australia. Repeating a miscalculation reminiscent of Hideyoshis attempted invasions of China in the 16th century, during late 1941 Japan launched a surprise naval and aerial attack on the United States territory at Pearl Harbor, Hawaii. The attack was triggered in response to US embargos over oil and the materials that fueled Japans war machine. Pearl Harbor attack, December 7, 1945 though its naval forces were weakened by the Pearl Harbor attack, the US forces fought back with unexpected resolve all across the Pacific islands. Despite fierce and bloody resistance from the Japanese military (employing in the final stages masses of suicide planes known as kamikaze), Japans ambitions of empire were ended in August 1945, as the US and the Soviet Union competed to accept the Japanese surrender in northeast East Asia. The final outcome was decided by the controversial use by the United States of the newly created atomic bomb on the cities of Nagasaki and Hiroshima, with massive civilian casualties. Post-War Japan was occupied for seven years (1945-1952) by Allied Forces under the leadership of General Douglas MacArthur of the United States. During this period a new, democratic constitution (ending Japans military role the world) was adopted, business re-oriented to peacetime objectives, and the country re-built itself (like other areas in East Asia) after the devastating war. In an interesting twist, the economy was stimulated by the Korean War, when the US forces took out contracts for military goods. Groups of Japanese engineers visited US companies in a systematic effort to modernize production, much as they had learned earlier from China and the West in earlier periods.

FIND YOURSELF

Through hard work and determination, Japan re-invented itself in the latter-half of the twentieth century as a consumer-oriented producer. It early on took the lead in transistor electronics and innovative automobile design (which benefited from traditional Japanese aesthetics), and by the late 1980s was the largest creditor nation on earth, while the US was the largest debtor. With the spread of film, radio, computer games and other electronic devices, Japanese popular culture has a worldwide influence. Japans growth became a model and stimulus for Hong Kong, Taiwan, Singapore, South Korea, Southeast Asia, and eventually the Peoples Republic of China (and possibly North Korea, in the future). Although old wounds sometimes still surfaced, a new age of growth and prosperity had arrived in East Asia by the late 1980s. Though plagued with a stagnant economy since the burst of the economic bubble in 1989 and increasingly cognizant of the problems of a graying society in which over 21% will soon be over age 65, Japan thru out the century remains a unique and vibrant cultural "Honor System", now in the 21st century, dealing with the dynamic cultures of China and Korea as the history of East Asia continues to unfold.

"I'm not
a product of my circumstances.
I'm a product of my
Decisions."

The darkness of Men is rented
by noise and flame. Men's souls
will be shaken with the violence of War.
For Men are drawn from
the ways of peace. They fight not for
the lust of control. They fight to end
conquest. They fight to liberate, to let
justice arise for endurance and good will
for all Men. They yearn for
the end of Battle,
to return to
Heaven
on
" EARTH "

~ Dr. Anthony Martin ~